Disclaimer: The opinions presented herein are solely those of the author except where specifically noted. Nothing in the book should be construed as investment advice or guidance, as it is not intended as investment advice or guidance, nor is it offered as such. Nothing in the book should be construed as a recommendation to buy or sell any financial or physical asset. It is solely the opinion of the writer, who is not an investment professional. The strategies presented in the book may be unsuitable for you, and you should consult a professional where such consultation is appropriate. The publisher/author disclaims any implied warranty or applicability of the contents for any particular purpose. The publisher/author shall not be liable for any commercial or incidental damages of any kind or nature.

First edition published October 2015

Oftwominds.com
P.O. Box 4727
Berkeley, California 94704

Interior: Jill Kanter
Cover: Theresa Barzyk
Concept: G.F.B.

A Radically Beneficial World: Automation, Technology and Creating Jobs for All

The Future Belongs to Work That Is Meaningful

Charles Hugh Smith

Table of Contents

Introduction

Up until recently, millions of us have prospered in ways previous generations only dreamed about. I'm not referring to owning mansions, yachts or buying political power — I mean *leading a self-directed life and owning the sources of our prosperity*.

This autonomy and ownership is known as *The American Dream*: the building of lasting value by doing work you care about, on your own terms.

We achieved this prosperity without the advantages of an Ivy League education or an inheritance. In other words, widespread prosperity flowed not from privilege or genius or luck, but from plentiful opportunities.

The system itself provided these opportunities. Millions of us stepped forward and seized them.

Fast-forward to today and times have changed: the opportunities of the recent past are distant memories. We all sense this, but don't know how to fix this new poverty of opportunity—to not just get ahead, but to *own* your work.

Defenders of the current order claim this decline is temporary, and modest reforms can fix whatever's broken.

But their denial doesn't change the reality that wages/salaries have been stagnating for decades while wealth/income inequality has soared. I won't bore you with the statistics, but anyone who looks at labor's share of the economy, earned income adjusted for inflation, or yardsticks of inequality realizes this isn't a temporary rough patch: the system itself is broken.

Even the defenders don't deny the global impact of automation on human labor, or the increasing demands on the Earth's resources as more than 7 billion people strive for middle-class consumption of food, energy, shelter and transport.

Optimists claim solar-powered electricity will soon be essentially free for everyone, but this doesn't mean that oceans stripped of sea life will magically be restored, or the forests cut to grow animal feed can be replaced with artificial trees. Refusing to recognize planetary limits doesn't make them go away.

Automation—software, robotics and artificial intelligence—is rapidly replacing human labor everywhere—and not just low-skilled work. As tech visionary Marc Andreessen famously noted, software is "eating the world." More to the point, software is eating paid work in greater and greater gulps every day.

This destruction of work will lead to a work-free Utopia, we're told, paid for by taxes on the owners of software and robots. But if we do the math—which we do in Chapter One—we discover this is absolutely baseless nonsense, the worst sort of magical thinking. Not a single wishful-thinker proclaiming the wonders of a guaranteed income for all in a work-free society has offered even a crayon sketch of where the money will come from using real-world sources such as corporate profits and federal tax revenues.

When it comes to understanding our socio-economic system, we're like fish in the sea: we cannot imagine any other system than the one we inhabit. We assume it's not just *the only system*, but that it's *the best system*: whatever its flaws might be, it has worked well in the past and it will work well in the future.

This is demonstrably false. Rather than being perfected over hundreds of years, our system is a junk heap of history: bits and pieces that happened to survive plagues, wars and revolutions. If we look at it with fresh eyes, this junk heap makes no sense whatsoever. It wasn't planned to be coherent, so no wonder it's incoherent. How could it not be?

The current system is based on five principles we assume are like socio-economic gravity, i.e. they're self-evidently true:

- Money created by banks trickles down to create work and wealth for all
- Technology always creates more jobs than automation destroys
- Centralization is the solution to large-scale economic problems
- Expanding debt and consumption (i.e. growth) is the path to prosperity

- Maximizing private gain organizes the economy to the benefit of all

If we look at these statements with fresh eyes, we realize they're all just wishful thinking. All five have proven to be untrue. Rather than being the foundation of a coherent system, each one adds more incoherence. Instead of serving as a solution, each one is a toxic problem that further erodes the system from within.

What does this system failure mean for us as individuals and households? For starters, anyone who wants a better future for themselves and their family needs to start taking charge of their destiny like never before.

But working within the failing system to better our individual destinies is no longer enough. Even the few who can afford to buy island fortresses will soon discover we share the consequences of the current system's failures. Once the seas are stripped of wildlife, they're stripped for everybody, not just the poor.

The real solution is obvious, isn't it? We need a new system. We all sense this, but don't know where to start. Let's begin with a simple question: *What if we could hit the reset button on the ways we create money, work, commerce and community?* If we could start from scratch, what would we build? This is not an idle question, for technology now enables us to hit that reset button and organize the creation of money, work, commerce and community in new ways.

If we set out to create a system that offers everyone the opportunity to control their own sources of prosperity, what would such a system look like?

If that's a question that interests you (and if it doesn't interest all of us, we're in real trouble), read on. This book lays out a complete, comprehensive global system-solution.

Its key is no secret: it is to understand *how systems work*.

Systems have inputs, rules and outputs. If we eat only jelly beans and never exercise, we become unhealthy because our bodies are a system:

Jelly beans + No Exercise = Poor Health and then Death

Simple!

In a similar way, our current economic/social/political system yields failing economic/social/political results.

To paraphrase a popular definition of insanity: "Insanity is feeding in the same inputs and expecting different results." Changing the flavors of the jelly beans and shifting positions on the sofa aren't going to change the end results (death).

Yet all the reforms that have been proposed so far are *exactly like changing the flavor of the jelly beans* and expecting this minor change to result in a fundamental improvement in our health.

We need an entirely new system if we want to change the output from inequality, insecurity and poverty to opportunity, secure work and prosperity.

This new system doesn't require overthrowing the existing order, or fixing the current system. This new system unifies existing technologies and social innovations that we can all understand. This new system is not utopian; it's extremely practical. We see examples of similar systems every day.

We don't want to keep failing by changing the flavor of our jelly beans and wondering why the results don't change. Change the system, and the outputs will become:

- opportunity
- autonomy
- secure work
- ownership of the sources of prosperity.

There is one planet-changing difference between our current system and the one described here. The current order is top-down, and to change anything, you need wealth and/or political power (if you have the wealth, you can buy the power). The individual is essentially powerless in this system; votes are counted but the top-down power structure remains unchanged.

In the system described in the pages to come, *every individual has the power to change the system for the betterment of themselves and every other participant.* Being at the top of the heap is no longer a prerequisite. Everyone who is powerless in the current arrangement is empowered in this new system. Empowered to not just better themselves and their family, but to better their community and through that organization, the larger community of Planet Earth.

My book embraces this global challenge in a great big bear-hug that snaps the shackles of ideological jargon and frees us to map a practical route to a radically beneficial future. What are we waiting for?

Section 1:

Why the Current System Has Failed

Chapter One: Gaping Holes in the Conventional Narrative

This book—originally titled *Bridging a Treacherous River: New Tools to Solve Global Poverty-*—started as a blueprint for alleviating global poverty. It was the culmination of my 40 years of pondering these simple questions: Is poverty inevitable? If not, what is the systemic solution that would alleviate poverty everywhere on the globe?

As a practical person by nature and training, I sought a practical answer.

I found we have two kinds of poverty: the age-old kind (scarcity) and a new kind driven by automation and software that is "eating the world," in Marc Andreessen's arresting phrase. Digital technologies are replacing human workers on a mass scale, threatening millions with a loss of income.

People who lose their livelihoods become poor not only in a financial sense, but also in purpose. The poverty extends far beyond their bank account into every aspect of their lives. A systemic solution to poverty has to solve both kinds of poverty.

Once the core cause of poverty is understood—a lack of secure paid work for all—I realized my real subject was *creating jobs for everyone who wanted paid work* - on a global scale. This was the solution not just for global poverty, but for automation's accelerating replacement of human labor.

In figuring out why *the only possible output of the current system is poverty and inequality*, I came to understand a few other things that will help us design a new system that outputs opportunity for all.

One is that state-capitalism (or whatever you want to label the current arrangement) is more than an economic or financial system; it organizes our relationships to Nature and other people, and does so without our really being aware of it.

In other words, a financial-economic system is also a social-political-resource-management system *by its very nature*. The design of the financial-money-economic system sets the course of everything else.

Secondly, the key to any financial-economic system is *value creation*. If a small group of people control the creation of value, the only possible output of the system is a poverty of opportunity and rising inequality—precisely what the current system yields.

By definition, money has value. Those who control the creation and distribution of value (i.e. money) control everything else downstream. If you don't change the way money is created and distributed, you haven't really changed anything. You're just eating a different color of jelly bean.

Let's say a system recognizes jelly beans as money. I own the only jelly bean factory and imprison everyone who tries to set up a competing jelly bean factory. Who do you think will be wealthy and powerful in this system? What is the only possible output of this system?

This is a simplification, of course, but you get the point. Those who control the creation of value control everything else. If we don't change the way money is created and distributed, nothing changes. We're just changing the color of jelly beans and wondering why the results don't change.

Opportunity boils down to *opportunity to create value*. If value creation is controlled by the few at the top of the heap, the many will lack opportunity. There is no other possible output of such a system.

We're all for freedom, of course. Only despots and dictators are against freedom. But freedom without opportunity to create value is illusory. What precisely does freedom mean in a system where value creation and opportunity are limited to the few at the expense of the many?

Chairman Mao famously claimed that "political power grows out of the barrel of a gun." The power of coercion grows out of the barrel of a gun, but that's not the same thing as political power, or the power to get things done.

It turns out Chairman Mao was wrong. *Cooperation is the basis of power.* The fellow in the jaunty Mao cap with the gun can only hold whatever power grows out of the gun barrel as long as he is pointing the gun at those with no guns. Coercion is a very limited form of power. Coercion doesn't create value, *cooperation creates value.*

9

We can only value what we measure. If we don't measure it, it doesn't exist. When we talk about inequality, we end up talking about money, because we can measure money. The end result of measuring inequality with money is the idea that if we give people a bit more money, inequality diminishes.

But inequality isn't really about money. Inequality is about who controls value creation and who has the opportunity to create value. Giving people money assuages the guilt of those at the top of the heap, but that's not actually changing the inequality of the system. It may buy the silence of those deprived of opportunity, but it doesn't change the sources of inequality.

Since we don't measure the sources of inequality, we don't even recognize them. If we deprive a person of the opportunity to create value, to actively contribute to something positive and important, but reckon a handout of money will make inequality go away, we're blind to the sources of inequality.

The first step is to recognize that money is not the only or even the most useful measure of inequality or value. It's not even an adequate measure of *capital*, because the most valuable capital is the opportunity to create value by freely cooperating with others.

The current system is a centralized hierarchy. Centralized hierarchies work great for those at the top of the wealth/ power/ security/ opportunity pyramid. The top 10% with most of the wealth, power, security and opportunity look down and declare that since the system works for them, it works for everyone. They gaze at the few who clamber up the pyramid to join their ranks as proof the system works for everyone with the right stuff: smarts, dedication, and so on.

Needless to say, these same people hold the wealth and power, so they're not about to let anyone else change the system lest they lose their spot on the top of the pyramid. Since they're smart, dedicated, etc., they can easily conjure up a limitless list of reasons why the system is sound and needs only modest reforms.

But whether the top 10% recognize it or not, or like it or not, the system is unjust. It is morally rotten to the core. Any system in which *the only possible output is poverty of opportunity and inequality* is rotten to the core.

But the system's moral corruption isn't the most pressing problem. The truly pressing problem is the five dictates listed in the introduction are eroding the system from within. The more we pursue these five dictates, the more we hollow out the system from within.

This leaves us with a choice. We can defend the rightness of the system that works for us as individuals, enabling us to maximize our private gains. We can eat different colored jelly beans and hope the system will magically save itself, or we can grasp the nettle and design a new system from the ground up that yields opportunity for all.

We're told there is always middle ground, but that's not always true. Sometimes it's either/or.

Going forward, let's focus on this truth: *a system that works for everyone works for us, too.*

Why Do We Reject New Solutions?

Our first reaction to any new solution is generally skepticism. There is more to this than just healthy *buyer beware* caution, and we need to understand the psychology of skepticism if we want to avoid falling into the trap of naysaying.

Skepticism is part of our intellectual immune system, protecting us from wishful thinking, fuzzy logic and the illusion of understanding (i.e. the urge to distill everything into a Power Point presentation).

But skepticism is also a cover for naysaying. Under the guise of skepticism, naysayers find ample fault with the present arrangement but even more in proposed solutions. When naysayers rule, the system stagnates. In companies, stagnation leads to bankruptcy. In societies, stagnation leads to a decline in vitality and the ability to solve problems.

Naysayers feel they're performing a valuable, even heroic duty in shooting down solutions. Thanks to their efforts, foolish people who might otherwise take unwarranted risks are saved from themselves.

That the naysayers themselves pose the greatest risk does not occur to them. Yet this is the reality. Nassim Taleb and others have shown that systems that resist the ferment of new solutions become increasingly brittle and fragile. Rejecting solutions guarantees systemic collapse.

One powerful reason we naysay is to protect our pay, perquisites, position and social standing from the threat posed by new solutions. Experimentation and competition are threats to vested interests, and we all understand the motivation to protect our share of the pie from the threat posed by *faster, better, cheaper*.

The common good is served not by self-serving vested interests but by *faster, better, cheaper*. If experimentation and competition are suppressed to protect vested interests, the system rots from within.

Naysaying triumphs when self-interest trumps the common good. Unsurprisingly, this depreciation of civic virtue in favor of self-interest— *maximizing personal gain* by whatever means are available—has been identified as a core cause of Rome's decline and fall.

Naysayers tend to find homes in Naysaying Organizations (NO) such as bureaucracies and monopolies—organizations that either exist to say no (bureaucracies) or that depend on the elimination of new solutions (also known as competition).

It's not accidental that Naysaying Organizations are centralized hierarchies. As we shall see Chapter Two, systems self-destruct when they get big, complex, centralized and hierarchical. How they self-destruct is simple: innovation, experimentation, competition are stifled as threats, and so *faster, better, cheaper* is safely buried in a shallow grave.

The way to get ahead in these organizations is to excel in naysaying— but do so while proclaiming your undying support of innovation. Innovation is fine as a principle, of course, but once it threatens vested interests, which ahem, it always does, it's quickly sent to the *further study is needed* graveyard.

Naysayers display their expertise not by innovating but by poking holes in others' innovations. Innovating is risky, naysaying is safe—especially in organizations that avoid risk. As a result, naysayers are praised by colleagues for protecting the organization from the threat of innovation.

There's another powerful motivation for naysaying. Those in the top 10%--the technocrat/financial layer of the economy—look at their own success and think, *the system works for me and my colleagues, so it's obviously working great.* The possibility that the system only works for the top 10%, or that this success is only temporary, is less persuasive than the personal experience of those within Naysaying Organizations.

In other words, when the system isn't working for you personally, you have little motivation to naysay. You're interested in solutions and are willing to give them a chance. But those safely protected by vested interests have many motivations to naysay and few reasons to support potentially disruptive solutions.

By all means, let's be skeptical, but let's also avoid the naysaying slide to stagnation and collapse.

My Personal Journey to the Solution

This book follows philosopher Ludwig Wittgenstein's memorable advice: "Don't get involved in partial problems, but always take flight to where there is a free view over the whole single great problem, even if this view is still not a clear one."
To my surprise, my own circuitous career path helped me identify the gaping holes in the conventional narratives and map out a new solution.

Here's a rough sketch of my career jumble: carpenter/builder, entrepreneur, employer, political activist, community volunteer, co-founder of a local non-profit, backroom manager of a small financial research company, and, more recently, self-employed author and writer in the digital marketplace of books, blogs and ideas. I've built a lot of houses and written a lot of books, and pickaxed an independent livelihood out of the trenches of the risk economy.

Steve Jobs gave a commencement speech at Stanford University in 2005 that's famous for its hard-won wisdom on the way our career dots only connect when we reach the point where it all comes together.

This book is that point.

Each of my work experiences contributed something to the dot-connecting that is irreplaceable. I would not have the same analytic tools in hand if even one of these were missing.

It's only fair to warn you that while learning carpentry as a young man I also earned a degree in philosophy. This means I occasionally have an irresistible urge to use an obscure word like *teleology*. I'm not trying to be obscure, I'm trying to be concise; sometimes a single word corrals a whole slew of important ideas.

Teleology is one such word. It means the end-goal, the end-point to which all the things we've done—successes *and failures*—were leading us.

There's teleology in our lives and in systems. What we'll be exploring in this book is how systems lead to specific end-points *by the nature of their design*.

Understanding abstractions is essential but insufficient. It's not enough to have abstract knowledge; you must combine it with boots-on-the-ground experience to understand how things really work.

There's one other essential ingredient: *risk*.

You can never really understand how things work unless you have skin in the game, and having skin in the game introduces risk. Losing, failing, being rejected, not getting paid—these focus our minds. There is no substitute for what we learn by grinding through real-world problems and facing the consequences.

Put abstract knowledge together with real-world knowledge, and if we're lucky, we develop an ability to think independently, to ask questions and come up with answers that aren't just snatched from accepted-wisdom narratives.

What's Easy but Guaranteed to Fail: Wishful Thinking

We all know that humans like things to be easy. We're designed that way for a reason. Calories are scarce in the hunter-gatherer world, and spending precious energy on difficult tasks has no pay off unless the rewards are outsized. (Recall that our brains are fierce furnaces that burn lots of calories.)

This is why we prefer wishful thinking to analysis. Wishful thinking is a lot less work. If given a choice, we'll opt for wishful thinking, as it's generally less risky that gambling precious energy on work that might not have a payoff.

But if we face difficult problems, wishful thinking isn't very useful because it doesn't generate solutions. Wishful thinking satisfies our preference for ease, but it doesn't solve problems.

If you're running a real enterprise, i.e. one that will bankrupt you if you fail to solve problems, wishful thinking is catastrophic. There are few guarantees in life, but wishful thinking guarantees failure.

Wishful thinking cannot replace the hard work of analysis, experimentation, and all the risky flailing of problem-solving.

So if we want to actually solve the problems of poverty and automation eating at our world, let's grit our teeth and perform some painfully calorie-gorging analysis. The results will be worth it.

Three Starting Points

Before we can start designing a new system, we first need to understand why the current system has failed. Otherwise, we may end up with the same result. Let's start with these three points:

1. The conventional narrative of our socio-economic system is so full of holes it no longer makes sense.
2. We're not asking the right questions - the ones that really need to be asked.
3. Systems are not ideological. They function independently of our wishes and cannot be fixed by mental or emotional trickery.

Though we're supposedly taught to think critically, amazingly little independent thinking is actually applied to the five narratives listed in the Introduction. Why is this so? There are several reasons.

If these narratives no longer make sense, we have to generate new ones. That is an inherently risky project, as the new narratives might be as incoherent as the current ones.

Though we really have no choice—the existing narratives make no sense, whether we like it or not—we avoid questioning the status quo because asking questions requires us to accept that the future is in doubt, and that uncertainty generates anxiety.

Another reason we don't ask the questions that need to be asked is a *failure of imagination*: few can imagine a world much different from the system we currently inhabit.

The idea that systems exist independent of ideology was sparked by a Donella Meadows essay, *Leverage Points: Places to Intervene in a System* (you can read it on donellameadows.org).

Prior to reading this essay, I accepted the conventional narrative that economic and social systems were ideological: capitalism, Marxism, democracy, socialism, and so on. People believed in the system or rejected it for ideological reasons.

That systems can be broken down into inputs, rules and outputs that have nothing to do with our beliefs about their goodness or efficacy was a revelation. Simply put, systems succeed or fail independently of our ideological convictions about the system.

Though the psychology of beliefs is complicated, it boils down to identity: our belief in a system's value is core to our identity.

We believe in the goodness and rightness of subsidized housing, for example, because we believe in social justice and housing for all. That it doesn't help low-income people is counter-intuitive and unacceptable: it must help low-income people because we want to help low-income people.

Similarly, we believe that maximizing private gain guides the system to prosperity because we believe in economic freedom. How could anyone not see the goodness and rightness of economic freedom? That maximizing private gain destroys the system is counter-intuitive and unacceptable: maximizing private gain must make the system function properly because self-interest is the core of liberty.

And so on. Every ideological belief can be broken down in this fashion.

We resist this analysis because it challenges our identity. No wonder we resist: what is more core to our sense of self than the beliefs that anchor our identity?

Once we understand this, we can separate our beliefs from systems. We can maintain our beliefs but understand that the system's success or failure has nothing to do with our convictions.

If we want positive output, we must examine the system as a system, not as an expression of our identity and beliefs.

Strangely, we insist on supporting systems whose outputs are precisely opposite to what we profess because we feel that an uncritical belief is an expression of our conviction.

That leaves us with a stark choice. We either set a goal of designing a system that produces a positive output, or we indulge our ideological beliefs. It's one or the other.

As Meadows points out, systems are often counter-intuitive: we intend them to yield a specific output, but the rules and inputs we choose may yield a completely different output than we expected. Add in a failure to imagine a world different from the one we inhabit, and it's no wonder our systems are self-destructing.

The first section of this book has three goals:

1. Examine the gaping holes in the conventional narrative that render it incoherent
2. Ask the questions that need to be asked but aren't being asked
3. Understand our economy/society as a system

Once we've accomplished these goals, we will be ready to design a system that actually produces a positive output.

Automation, Jobs and Guaranteed Income

In researching what others have proposed as solutions to automation, I was astonished to find gaping holes in the conventional narrative of what happens as software and robots replace vast swaths of human labor. The conventional narrative (as presented by highly regarded economists, academics, journalists and public intellectuals) is that automation's inevitable erosion of jobs will result in either:

- The creation of even more jobs than those lost to advancing technology; or
- A guaranteed minimum income for all, funded by taxes on those who own the robots and software that ate all the jobs.

17

In other words, *we don't need to change the inputs or the system:* the system will solve the wholesale destruction of jobs without us having to do anything different. It will automatically create more jobs than it destroys, and the state will collect more taxes and pay everyone a minimum income.

That each of these conclusions is incoherent and impractical is clear to anyone with entrepreneurial experience and a basic grasp of government spending and corporate profits.

Let's start with the idea that technology will always create more jobs than it destroys.

There is little evidence that this is still true. It may have been true in the past, but not now.

When asked to name one technology that has created more jobs than it destroyed in the past decade, the typical answer is biotechnology. But what few seem to recall is that the chemistry-based pharmaceutical industry was gutted by the rise of the bio-based pharmaceuticals; thousands of jobs were lost. The stunning lack of profitability of the vast majority of biotechs is also not mentioned; nor is the surplus of workers trained in science, technology, engineering and math (STEM).

Issuing more STEM degrees doesn't create jobs for the graduates.

This faith that technology will magically create more jobs than it destroys is wishful thinking. This theology arose as a result of the transition from low-skill agricultural labor to low-skill factory labor in the First Industrial Revolution (1750 – 1860, steam, railways, factories, etc.) and the Second Industrial Revolution (1870-1930) (mass production, electric lights, autos, aircraft, radio, telephones, movies). Each transition offered millions of new low-skill jobs to those displaced by technology and created increasing numbers of higher-skill jobs in design, technology, marketing and management. But history is not repeating itself in the latest Industrial revolution.

The Third Industrial Revolution

This latest revolution began with digital communications and data-processing, and has lately witnessed rapid advances in robotics,

18

software and networked digital devices, i.e. the World Wide Web and the Internet of Things.

For the first time in the progression of technology, there are no low-skill jobs being created by the latest revolution. Not only are there few low-skill jobs created by the digital revolution, existing high-skill jobs are being eroded by rapid advances in artificial intelligence and software.

Since automation/software is now eating higher-skill jobs, advancing the skills of workers does not automatically create jobs for them. Pushing the entire populace to get a college diploma does not automatically create jobs that require college diplomas.

The conventional narrative overlooks a key dynamic in the Third Industrial Revolution: *the number of skilled workers needed to eliminate entire industries of highly skilled employees is much smaller than the workforces being eliminated.*

Craigslist, for example, has fewer than 50 employees but single-handedly wiped out thousands of middle-class jobs that were once supported by classified advertising in the print media.

Coding software—what many still see as the engine of future job growth—is itself being automated. Teaching everyone how to program will not automatically create millions of new jobs as machines take over many labor-intensive parts of programming.

In many cases, programming is already a process of grabbing chunks of code from online libraries and stitching them together: drag-and-drop replaces cumbersome coding. In other cases, automated systems such as MIT's Helium can clean up and optimize legacy code in an hour, a project that could take months of human labor.

In a world of global competition and tight budgets, a program that can do the work of dozens of humans in a few hours (and do it better) is manna from heaven.

Two features of automated programming help us understand why the Third (Digital) Industrial Revolution is different from the previous two Industrial Revolutions.

1. The work of writing the code will not have to be repeated. It only needs to be written once. Once it has been created, the

program will chew through thousands of lines of legacy software code automatically, learning more as it goes along.
2. A digital copy can be distributed globally at near-zero cost.

These features help us understand why automated programming will not create more highly paid jobs for humans than it destroys: the entire purpose of automated software is to dramatically lower costs and improve output by eliminating human labor and the costs of delivery and operation.

Human Labor Is the $450 Option, Automation is the $45 Option

The faith that technology will create more jobs than it destroys is understandable. The standard narrative has only two mechanisms for creating jobs: profit-maximizing enterprises and government. If these sectors cannot create jobs more jobs than technology destroys, the standard narrative has no solution.

Mainstream economists are gingerly exploring this job-destroying black hole. Erik Brynjolfsson, Andrew McAfee and Nobel Prize winning economist Michael Spence wrote in 2014 that "Should the digital revolution continue to be as powerful in the future as it has been in recent years, the structure of the modern economy and the role of work itself may need to be rethought."

Though they were careful not to predict the digital revolution will continue at its current pace, the reality is that the revolution is picking up speed. Rather than hope software will lose its appetite for eating up jobs, we can anticipate its appetite will only increase.

Why is this so?

Jobs are not created by magic or by abstract theories. Jobs are created one at a time, by offering someone else a paycheck to perform work that is profitable. If software can perform the work faster, better and cheaper than a human, it makes no financial sense to pay a human to do the work.

Only employers fully grasp the impact of digital technologies on job creation, because they're the only ones who have to ask: does hiring another employee make financial sense?

The vast majority of the workforce are employees, and have no experience being an employer. This places an *experiential limit* on our collective understanding of the realities of creating jobs. What sounds plausible in the abstract to those with no experience of payroll expenses outrunning income (i.e. losing money) is often impractical in the real world.

In the real world, hiring more employees could bankrupt you and your enterprise.

The mainstream media glorifies the very few at the top of the entrepreneurial food-chain who reap billions in profits, but in the trenches of the risk economy, it's difficult to earn a profit. In this world, staying alive requires reducing human labor or extracting more value from each employee.

Capitalism's core function is to generate profit and expand capital. Creating jobs is not the core purpose of capitalism, nor is it the government's core purpose. We take it for granted that employment will expand as a secondary effect of capital and the state (i.e. government) pursuing their core purposes, but in the digital global economy, this can no longer be taken for granted.

The reality is that enterprises and states have to adopt labor-saving technologies to survive. Confirmation can be found by simply scanning current headlines: the U.S. Navy is looking at 3-D fabrication of ships (not components, *entire ships*), Chinese manufacturers turn to fully automated factories, self-driving trucks take to the road, and even jobs that seem too low-tech for robotics such as harvesting tea leaves are being automated.

Automation is not an option that can be rejected in favor of business as usual. As we shall see in a moment, automation is the inescapable result of structural forces that only grow stronger. Chief among these is the rising cost of human labor—not just in developed countries, but everywhere.

There is a widespread sense of disbelief that automation can eat high-skill, middle-class jobs in the same way that it ate low-skill agricultural and factory jobs. In this view, the 50 employees of Craigslist wiping out thousands of middle-class jobs in the classified ad industry was a fluke.

But the reality is that the strongholds of middle-class jobs—for example, healthcare, education, government, and national defense—are all increasingly unaffordable and therefore ripe for wholesale creative destruction of costs, jobs and business as usual.

The conventional solution to rising costs in these industries is to raise taxes or borrow more money. But taxes can only go so high before they trigger recessions and other self-correcting mechanisms. Borrowing money eventually bankrupts the borrower, no matter how big. Is borrowing another trillion dollars an actual solution to soaring college costs?

These aren't sustainable solutions; they're wishful thinking.

The solution is to lower costs with technology—not by 3% or 5%, but by 50% or 90%.

Those earning a living in these unaffordable sectors defend the status quo by claiming that humans do a better job than machines and software, or that humans are essential, regardless of their cost.

In many cases, this is self-serving wishful thinking.

As for disregarding costs: *what we can afford is good enough.* As an example, an Apple iPad costs $450. A tablet running the free Android operating system sells for $45 (10% of the iPad's cost) in China and India. Yes, the iPad has some advantages over the $45 tablet. But what are the advantages worth to those can't afford the iPad? What are the *opportunity costs* of opting for the product that costs 10 times more than the commoditized version? In other words—what else could have been done with the $405 saved by buying the cheap tablet? What else could have been done with the interest paid to borrow the additional $405?

Research suggests children given tablets with games designed to teach them to read and write learn to read and write without any teacher at all. A teacher may be a plus, but if you can't afford one, a cheap tablet with instructional games does the job.

The more we learn about what makes education truly effective, the easier it is to automate those processes into software that works on $45 tablets.

We can't be blamed for priding our human capacity for empathy and insight. These are valuable capacities. But if all we can afford is a $45 tablet, singing the praises of the iPad is not a solution.

There are already robots in classrooms and robots designed to care for the infirm elderly. There are robots that return the wheelchair-bound to mobility. Software already does much of the flying in advanced aircraft.

Diehards are ready to declare fighter pilots as essential regardless of the cost, but what if we can no longer afford $200 million-each fighter aircraft? *Regardless of the cost* is another way of saying *when somebody else is paying the bills* or *put it on the credit card*. Neither is a solution; both are wishful thinking.

If all we can afford is a robot caregiver, the solution becomes improving the robot's capabilities, not trying to replace it with a costly human. If all we can afford is a pilotless aircraft guided from the ground, the solution is not to borrow $1 trillion to build obsolete fighters that satisfy our desire to appear essential. The solution is to improve the pilotless aircraft's capabilities.

That unaffordable and inefficient systems should be replaced is both obvious and necessary, but we resist this because we recognize the jobs lost cannot be replaced.

Consider the way we currently handle medical tests. The patient drives to a clinic or hospital, waits in a room (a total waste of potentially productive time) while a vast bureaucracy processes the interaction and payment. A sample is taken and the patient drives back to work or home. The samples are shipped to a lab, where highly paid staff process them. Results are then entered in a system and distributed to the patient and the doctors/nurses.

All of this consumed costly fuel, time and labor. Even worse, the readings are snapshots that can be deceptive. What if hospitals make the patient anxious? (I raise my hand.) The patients' blood pressure reading will be higher than it is at home. The patient may be prescribed a medication that isn't really necessary.

Digital technology is enabling a much cheaper, more efficient way to handle tests. Patients wear digital devices that take continuous readings in real time. Smart phones are becoming monitoring devices that eliminate the travel, time and bureaucratic friction. There is no paperwork; the device sends data to caregivers digitally.

Claiming the current system is necessary and effective is absurd. It is clearly wasteful, unaffordable, inefficient and unnecessary.

Replacing it will eliminate far more jobs than are created in software development. There is no equivalent expansion of jobs, and no going back to high-cost, wasteful, inefficient systems that generated the jobs.

Roughly 50% of healthcare expenses in the U.S. are devoted to the 5% of the populace with multiple chronic diseases. If technology can reduce the costs of monitoring and treating these patients by eliminating human labor, we will eventually have no choice but to pursue this cost reduction. Putting the ballooning cost of healthcare on the national credit card is not a sustainable solution.

Higher education boils down to a simple premise: once a student learns how to learn, they don't need a complex bureaucracy to learn. As I outlined in my book *The Nearly Free University and the Emerging Economy*, a 90% reduction in higher education costs are not just possible but necessary.

Digital technologies enable radical reductions in cost and improvement in results.

Why pay 10,000 instructors to deliver middling-quality lectures when a superior lecture is online for free? Why maintain costly campuses and bureaucracies when most students don't even need to set foot on campus and lessons can be delivered without the bureaucracy?

All the justifications of the status quo in healthcare, education and national defense are the equivalent of hectoring the person with $50 to buy the $450 iPad instead of the $45 tablet. Insisting the person with $50 buy the $450 device because it might be marginally better is not a solution.

Perhaps the $1 trillion F-35 fighter aircraft is marginally better in certain circumstances, but aircraft piloted from the ground that cost 90% less are better in many other circumstances—a fact never mentioned by those defending their jobs in the status quo.

A sprawling campus and highly paid staff may be better than online learning linked with apprenticeships in certain circumstances, but in many other situations, learning within the directed apprenticeship model is far more effective than forcing students to sit through four years of lectures to earn an incredibly costly credential with rapidly depreciating real-world value.

At the risk of annoying those who dislike repetition: *Regardless of the cost* is another way of saying *when somebody else is paying the bills* or *put it on the credit card*. Neither is a solution.

Technology is eating skilled middle-class jobs the same way it ate low-skill jobs, and as a result of soaring costs, its appetite for middle-class jobs is growing. The jobs created by lower-cost technologies are themselves prone to automation once the initial development has been done.

Human labor is the $450 option, and saying it is essential doesn't help those with only $50. Their only rational choice is to buy the $45 option, and work on improving the output of that low-cost technology.

The Flaws in Guaranteed Income for All

Let's return to the second conventional solution in the narrative of what happens when automation eliminates huge swaths of paid human labor: a guaranteed minimum income is to paid to all, funded by taxes collected from those reaping profits from robots and software.

This is the *super welfare state solution*: the government collects enough taxes to pay social welfare benefits not just to the temporarily unemployed and those who cannot work (children, disabled and the elderly) but to the majority of citizens, not just during one phase of their lives, but for their entire lives.

The most obvious problem with this solution to mass unemployment is the math doesn't work: the owners of robots and software cannot make enough profit to pay the staggering costs of a guaranteed minimum income distributed to tens of millions of jobless households.

A quick look at current government spending and corporate profits illustrates the disconnection between the costs of guaranteed minimum income for all and reality.

The U.S. federal government currently spends $3.2 trillion annually, and roughly two-thirds of this is for programs such as Social Security (income security), Medicare, Medicaid, housing subsidies, SNAP (food stamps), unemployment and so on.

Estimating the cost of *guaranteed income for all* is difficult if we don't know the total number of households that will collect this benefit and the size of the benefit, but we can certainly anticipate the costs will be much higher than current spending.

State and local government spend another $3 trillion, so in total government spends over $6.2 trillion annually in the U.S. This is roughly 36% of America's $17 trillion gross domestic product (GDP). That's a lot of taxes that must be collected from enterprises and wage earners.

- Every person who loses their job to automation increases the cost of *guaranteed income for all*. If millions of people lose their jobs, the costs of *guaranteed income for all* will skyrocket.
- Every person who loses their job stops paying payroll and income taxes. If millions of people lose their jobs, government tax revenues plummet accordingly.

Total corporate profits in 2015 are about $1.8 trillion. If the government took every last dollar of corporate profit (which is obviously impractical), this is less than 30% of total government spending.

But—so goes the conventional thinking—digital companies will be even more profitable than the existing batch of companies.

Is this reality-based or just more wishful thinking?

Let's take three tech giants that virtually everyone holds up as positive examples of growth in the digital economy: Google, Facebook and Twitter.

Google has revenues of $70 billion (as of mid-2015), net income (profit) of $14 billion, and 55,000 employees worldwide. (Their U.S. based work force is around 33,000.)

If Google's entire net profit was taken by the federal government, we'd need 443 Googles, each reaping $14 billion a year to fund all government expenditures.

But there is only one Google on the planet, and there isn't enough oxygen for another Google, much less hundreds of equivalently profitable corporations. Google already handles the vast majority of web searches.

If we assume those 443 highly profitable corporations would each need 33,000 U.S. based employees to operate, we'd have about 15 million private employees—roughly 10% of the American workforce of 150 million.

Facebook has 10,000 employees globally and generated net income of $2.8 billion. We'd need 2,214 Facebooks to fund all government spending. Those 2,214 companies would have a workforce of 22 million employees—less than 20% of the workforce.

But there is only one Facebook on the planet, and an equivalent company or two in China. What the other 2,213 highly profitable digital companies going to do to generate billions in profits and employ 10,000 people?

Consider Twitter, with its global reach and 3,900 employees. Its earnings before interest, taxes, depreciation and amortization (EBITDA) are -$339 million. Yes, a loss. It's a growing company, so perhaps it will earn a net profit soon. But there are no guarantees of that.

So how many Twitter equivalents do we need to fund $6.2 trillion in government spending? If companies aren't highly profitable, there's nothing to tax. And if they don't have many employees (recall Craigslist's 50 employees), there won't be enough payroll to reap $6.2 billion in taxes.

In each of these cases, the company dominates its sector; there isn't enough oxygen for even one more Google, Facebook, Twitter or Craigslist, never mind thousands of such digital companies.

This is a very simple model, obviously, as I haven't counted taxes Google paid before net profit was calculated, the payroll taxes paid by the employees, and so on. But the point is that a guaranteed income that requires $7+ trillion of taxes needs highly profitable corporations and tens of millions of well-paid employees paying substantial taxes.

If neither of those conditions applies, then the guaranteed minimum income idea is impractical: as profits and jobs decline, so do taxes.

Whether we like it or not, the guaranteed minimum income solution to mass unemployment is just wishful thinking. Even the most profitable digital companies generate only a tiny slice of the profits and payrolls needed to fund guaranteed income for all, and they employ an equally tiny slice of the workforce.

And this is assuming there is never a recession—a very foolish assumption indeed!

In recessions, corporate profits tend to fall precipitously. Were profits to fall to $1 trillion (as they have in previous recessions), corporate taxes would barely cover 15% of current government expenditures—never mind that the cost of *guaranteed income for all* would soar as corporations slash payrolls.

Proponents of guaranteed income reckon increasing taxes on landlords, polluting industries, sugar and alcohol, etc. would pay for the added costs. The problem is there are already steep taxes on virtually all of these categories, and a quick glance at the actual profits each generates reveals that the increased taxes would fall far short of replacing all the tax revenues lost as profits decline and jobs vanish.

The only possible conclusion: guaranteed minimum income for all is *wishful thinking*.

But there's an even bigger hole in this narrative, as we shall see.

Automation Commoditizes Labor, Goods and Services, Slashing Profits

As automation eats jobs, it also eats profits, since automation turns labor, goods and services into commodities. When something is *commoditized*, the price drops because the goods and services are interchangeable and can be produced almost anywhere.

The $45 tablet can be assembled anywhere, and the software can be coded anywhere.

Big profits flow from scarcity, i.e. when demand exceeds supply. If supply exceeds demand, prices fall and profits vanish.

The cost of automation and robotics is falling dramatically. This lowers the cost of entry for smaller, hungrier, more nimble competitors, and lowers the cost of increasing production.

The parts needed to assemble a $45 tablet are dropping in price, and the profit margins on those parts is razor-thin because they're commodities. Software such as the Android operating system is free, and many of the software libraries need to assemble new software are also free.

Automation increases supply and lowers costs. Both are deadly to profits.

So here's the core problem with the idea that taxing the owners of robots and software will fund guaranteed incomes for all: *the more labor, goods and services are automated/commoditized, the lower the profits*.

The current narrative assumes more wealth will be created by the digital destruction of industries and jobs, but real-world examples suggest the exact opposite: the music industry has seen revenues fall in half as digital technology ate its way through the sector. A $14 billion industry is now a $7 billion industry. Profits and payroll taxes collected from the industry have plummeted.

As subscription music services replace sales of songs and albums, revenues will continue to decline even as consumers have greater access to more products. In other words, the destruction of sales, employment and profits is far from over.

Examples of such radical reductions abound in daily life. To take one small example, our refrigerator recently failed. The motor was running but the compartment wasn't being cooled. Rather than replace the appliance for hundreds of dollars or hire a high-cost repair service, I looked online, diagnosed the problem as a faulty sensor, watched a tutorial on YouTube (what I call *YouTube University*), ordered a new sensor for less than $20 online and completed the repair at no cost beyond a half-hour of labor, which cost me nothing in terms of cash spent.

The profit earned by YouTube was minimal, as was the profit of the firms that manufactured the sensor and shipped it. The sales and profits that were bypassed by using nearly-free digital tools were an order of magnitude higher.

I was recently interviewed via Skype by an online journalist with millions of views of his YouTube channel. A decade ago when he worked in mainstream TV journalism, an interview required costly, time-consuming travel (for the crew or the subject), a sound engineer, a camera operator, the talent (interviewer), editor and managerial review. These six jobs have been rolled into one with digital tools, and travel has been eliminated entirely.

Some will argue that the quality of the video and sound isn't as high, but the quality of the user experience is ultimately based on the viewer's display, which is increasingly a phone or tablet. So in terms of utility, value and impact, the product (i.e. *output*) produced by one person replaces the conventional media product that required six people.

My own solo digital content business would have required a handful of people (if not more) only a decade ago. With digital tools and services, it now requires just one person. Those of us who must work with digital tools to survive know firsthand that what once required a handful of workers must now be produced by one person if we hope to earn even a marginally middle-class income.

Multiply an appliance that doesn't need to be replaced and a repair service that doesn't need to be hired, a half-dozen positions replaced by one part-time job, a commodity device that costs 10% of the high-profit brand and you understand why profits will plummet as software eats the world.

These are not starry-eyed examples based on projections; these are real-world examples of digital technologies destroying costs, sales and profits on a massive scale.

Some observers have suggested taxing wealth rather than profits to fund the super welfare state. But the value of assets ultimately rests on their ability to generate a profit. As profits fall, wealth may be more chimerical than these observers believe.

The Rising Cost of Human Labor

There's another driver of automation the conventional narrative misses: the rising costs of human labor.

Unlike a human worker, a robot doesn't require healthcare insurance, worker's compensation, 401K pension benefits, and all the other costs of labor overhead. A robot doesn't go on strike for higher wages.

As socio-economist Immanuel Wallerstein has observed, the cost of labor is rising globally as a result of structural forces that are immune to productivity gains, recessions, tax credits or other factors:

1. Urbanization
2. External costs (environmental damage, etc.) that must now be paid
3. Rising payroll taxes as the public demands more services from the state

These trends are especially visible in China, which has seen wages soar, costs of pollution control soar and demands for state services soar.

So where does this leave us?

- Technology no longer creates more jobs than it destroys.
- Profits decline as automation commoditizes labor, goods and services globally.
- Digital and robotic tools are falling in price while the cost of human labor inexorably rises.
- As costs of automation plummet, barriers to entry fall and competition increases, pushing everyone into automation if they want to survive.

As profits fall and jobs are eliminated, the tax base narrows and the state collects less tax revenue. Even the state must automate to reduce costs.

Put all these together and the conclusion is inescapable: the conventional narrative solutions (belief that more jobs will be created than destroyed, guaranteed income for all) are wishful thinking.

The same can be said of calls for the state to hire tens of millions of displaced workers in a supersized *make work* program—where is the money going to come from as tax revenues falter?

Yes, government can borrow money, but this is not a sustainable way to fund tens of millions of jobs. If profits and job growth aren't coming back, borrowing money is a temporary stopgap, not a solution.

The System Can't Solve the Problems of Automation

Let's summarize what we've found so far in terms of systems.

The conventional narrative claims the current system will automatically create more jobs without us having to do anything different. And if this turns out to be false, then the system will give everyone a guaranteed income for life, without changing anything but the tax rate on the companies that own the robots and software that ate all the jobs.

Both solutions are completely impractical, with no basis in reality. Both are wishful thinking.

But that's not all that's wrong with the conventional system.

Poverty Is More than Material

The conventional narrative does not recognize that the loss of jobs includes a loss of purpose and social cohesion. In the fantasy version of guaranteed income, people receiving a guaranteed income are free to explore literature, compose music, create artwork, play games and live a life of productive leisure. Freed from the burden of work, people will consume the goods and services created by automation.

This fantasy overlooks the reality that communities that are given free housing, food and healthcare are breeding grounds for self-destructive pathologies, depression, ill-health and unhappiness. The public intellectuals who espouse the fantasy of creative leisure base their vision of Utopia on their own peer group, the most educated, most motivated, most accomplished and most ambitious 1% of the workforce. Most people are not able to sustain purpose and meaning outside a work environment that provides meaningful social roles.

Work is the foundation of purpose and positive social roles; leisure and consumption are not.

Researcher John B. Calhoun found that once the number of individuals capable of filling social roles exceeds the number of roles available, social cohesion breaks down, and the resulting pathology of shared hopelessness creates what Calhoun called a *behavioral sink*. Hope and the human spirit are both destroyed by this bottomless black hole.

Though we think of poverty in material terms, the deeper loss when jobs disappear is the loss of positive social roles, purpose and meaning—not just a reason to get up in the morning, but a reason to contribute. Simply giving people money does not automatically create positive social roles. Rather, it reinforces a self-destructive state I call *permanent adolescence* in which a focus on leisure and consumption trivializes human life. This stripping away of social roles in favor of consumerism leads to self-absorption and a loss of purpose, pride and meaning.

That economists are blind to the terrible impoverishment of human life when meaningful work disappears is astounding, and reminds us that *work isn't just a financial arrangement*; it is a social arrangement and a source of individual pride and purpose.

The loss of jobs is not just a loss of income but a poverty of opportunity to acquire ownership of the *engines of wealth creation.* People don't want to just get by; they want to get ahead. Giving them a free stipend robs them of the opportunity to do more than just scrape by.

Job loss dismantles not just incomes but the ecosystem of community that work and jobs construct. Take away the jobs and you get what author Yann Moulier-Boutang has called the "poverty of social organization."

The problem with guaranteed income isn't that it aims too high, but that it aims too low. Rather than empower people with secure jobs, it strips away social roles and opportunities that only work provides.

Growth Is Not a Sustainable or Positive Model

Yet another gaping hole is the assumption that growth—of consumption, production, sales, profits, wages and taxes—is the highest good because growth is presumed to raise all boats like an incoming tide.

This view made sense when resources were cheap and plentiful. But with 7 billion people aspiring to a middle-class life, there are constraints on resources. The oceans, for example, have already been stripped of many species. Depleted soil and fresh water aquifers cannot be restored if demands on these resources keep expanding.

The digital revolution is eating the world partly because it consumes fewer resources. For example:

- Rather than invest cement, steel and vast quantities of energy in constructing thousands of new hotel rooms, Airbnb makes thousands of new rooms available within existing buildings.
- Car sharing enables a number of people to have access to a vehicle without every person buying and maintaining a vehicle. This *access not ownership* model is a much more efficient and resource-stingy way of living, but by making better use of fewer vehicles, it kills the conventional god of growth.
- Music labels once shipped records or CDs to thousands of outlets; now listeners download digital files.
- Books that were once printed in mass quantities and shipped to retailers (who shipped unsold copies back to the publishers, who then shipped them out again to be remaindered) are now printed on demand: when a customer orders a copy, the book is printed and shipped (or delivered digitally at near-zero cost). All the wasted transport of the old model has been eliminated.
- Where a separate device was once required to listen to music, watch TV or open a spreadsheet, now a single mobile device does it all.

These are just a few examples of the way digital technologies reduce costs and growth as measured in sales, energy consumption, etc.

For a system that requires permanent growth, this is fatal. *Faster, better, cheaper* means fewer profits, fewer jobs, less consumption, and a narrowing tax base. Everyone focuses on the few companies that reap big profits from this destruction of established sectors, but few add up the profits and jobs lost.

The initial disruption reaps big profits, but this is a one-off: once the old way of doing things has been replaced, the big gains dwindle as the new technology is itself commoditized.

What's good for sustainability (lower consumption of resources, goods and labor) is fatal to the narrative of permanent growth.

There's another gaping hole in the *permanent growth is necessary* narrative. This narrative is based on the oft-repeated idea that human desires are limitless and therefore sales and profits can expand forever as these infinite desires are met by the production of more goods and services. But is this idea actually true?

Starting from a point of material deprivation, it seemed like wants were unlimited. But the core human needs are actually quite limited. Beyond the physical requirements of food, water and shelter (in Maslow's *hierarchy of needs*, the physiological necessities), human needs are intangible and cannot be filled by profit-maximizing companies or the state. The idea that human desires are limitless and can be profitably filled by more goods and services is impoverishing and adolescent. Human life is more than just the fulfillment of our desires.

For example, friendship is clearly a human need. Can a product replace friendship? No. Can friendship be bought or rented? No. What if consumerist superficialities have eroded our experience of real friendship in ways we have difficulty even detecting?

Permanent growth requires endless marketing of increasingly marginal goods and services. I call this process *the financialization of the human experience*: every human interaction and emotion is transformed into a financial transaction that benefits a profit-maximizing company, bank and the state, which needs financial transactions to generate its tax revenues.

To prompt the purchase of unneeded goods and services, marketing undermines the authentic self in favor of narcissism and self-gratification.

The process of permanent consumerist growth is simple:

- Generate insecurity and self-doubt by marketing impossible standards: only those who are thin, fit, super-smart, witty, personable, creative, wealthy and appropriately humble are worthy.
- Make buying a good or service the solution to inadequacy.

Creating insecurity that can only be resolved with impulsive purchases of signifiers generates the destructive state of *permanent adolescence*.

Once we scrape away the marketing and grasp the full consequences, we realize that the ideology of permanent growth is a disaster, not just for the overburdened planet but for every individual and culture ensnared by this perverse fantasy.

The entire narrative of unlimited desires driving ever-expanding growth and profits is not only false, it is counter-productive. The focus on marketing unnecessary goods and services that fill our most adolescent desires and insecurities actively inhibits our fulfillment of the intangible needs of friendship, reciprocity, belonging, purpose, positive social roles and empathy.

The Knowledge Economy and Cognitive Capitalism

Phrases like *knowledge economy* and *cognitive capitalism* cause our eyes to glaze over.

What do they mean? Do they refer to something real, or are they just academic abstractions?

What they describe is real, but maddeningly ambiguous, as things aren't always as cut and dried as we'd like in the middle of revolutions—in this case, the Third (Digital) Industrial Revolution.

So let's burn some calories figuring out what these terms mean in the real world.

What authors Moulier-Boutang and McKenzie Wark term the *knowledge economy* (or *cognitive capitalism* in Boutang's phrase) is a different system from hierarchically-organized corporations, states and labor.

In this new arrangement, the once-sharp lines separating ownership, labor and assets blur, and production is no longer limited to conventional labor making things or providing services. Cognitive labor, in the form of research and development, logistical management, etc., fuels the transformation of intellectual activities into tradable assets.

Value is generated by the *network*, a new organizational form that is unlike the traditional hierarchies of corporations and states. Economist Michael Spence (among others) has observed that value (in the form of assets and profits) flows to what's scarce.

- Since automation and software excel at turning processes into commodities, commoditized goods/services create very little value/profit.
- Since central banks have pushed the cost of credit to near-zero, capital is easily borrowed for next to nothing and consequently it also has little scarcity value.

The value in the knowledge economy is not just any knowledge, but knowledge that increases productivity, which we can summarize as *faster, better, cheaper* and *doing more with less*.

Productivity depends on innovation, which is itself dependent on collaborative skills and cross-fertilization of various knowledge bases.

As Spence and co-authors Andrew McAfee and Erik Brynjolfsson observed in their 2014 essay, *Labor, Capital and Ideas in the Power Law Economy*, neither capital nor labor have scarcity value in the age of automation and nearly-free credit. "Fortune will instead favor a third group: those who can innovate and create new products, services, and business models."

Value in the knowledge economy is not distributed equally. The returns on human labor and capital are very low, while the scarcity of skills and knowledge that create new business models drives most of the gains to the creative class: "The distribution of income for this creative class typically takes the form of a power law, with a small number of winners capturing most of the rewards. In the future, ideas will be the real scarce inputs in the world -- scarcer than both labor and capital -- and the few who provide good ideas will reap huge rewards."

In his *Information Theory of Capitalism*, author George Gilder proposed that the economy is fundamentally a system that rewards learning and knowledge. Its conventional features—investing capital wisely and distributing wealth—are secondary. Commentator Bill Bonner offered this explanation: "Information, says Gilder, is always surprising. It tells us things we didn't know. The person who is the source of most important new information is the entrepreneur."

Learning is difficult and costly. Developing new ideas and applying them in the real world is a risky, uncertain process. From this perspective, rewards flow not just to what's scarce but to what's risky. Since most ideas fail to reach fruition, new ideas that succeed are intrinsically scarce.

In other words, there is no risk-free way to identify and exploit scarcity in a knowledge economy.

The value in work is identifying what's scarce, which increasingly includes intangibles such as *attention and care*. Collaboration, responsiveness, autonomy and inventiveness—core skills in the creative class of cognitive capitalism—are difficult to measure in traditional terms.

What is the hourly rate for autonomy and inventiveness?

The rewards depend on the value of the output, which is intrinsically unpredictable.

If we understand risk and scarcity, we understand why the traditional model of paying people for their time no longer makes any sense. Even paying people for their skills makes no sense, since there is no guarantee that these skills will generate new ideas that create value.

This leaves us with a sobering realization: there is no hourly rate for autonomy and inventiveness. The value depends entirely on the output of the work.

The knowledge economy richly rewards cognitive *piecework*—being paid for what was accomplished, not the time spent performing the work. But unlike the conventional factory model, the value of the work isn't known in advance, since the most valuable products are not new ideas but *new ideas that reach fruition*.

Ownership of the new ideas is not the same as ownership of mines, ships and factories, as new ideas can be digitally distributed for free.

In his 1993 book *Post-Capitalist Society*, Peter Drucker identified the worker's knowledge as the *means of production* in the knowledge economy.

In the traditional economy, the means of production were assets such as factories that hired labor by the hour to produce goods and services. This division alienated the worker from the value of his labor. The knowledge economy reconnects the rewards with the owners of the new means of production: the cognitive creators themselves.

The network offers new ways to organize work and produce value. Centralized hierarchies are no longer needed to manage workers and tasks; self-directed creators collaborate on projects and share income streams without a managerial hierarchy overseeing their work.

If we follow Christopher Lasch's analysis of commoditization in his book *The Culture of Narcissism*, we find that it's not just employees who are interchangeable--employers are equally interchangeable. The interchangeability of work, employees, employers, products and services is the key characteristic of commoditization.

If you find all this frustratingly imprecise, I share your frustration. Even though I work in the knowledge economy and am living in the world of cognitive capitalism, I am hard-pressed to make sense of my work or value in conventional terms such as hourly rates.

Even though this framework of value creation defies easy quantification, it doesn't mean it is any less real than traditional economic structures. Yes, the world still needs manufactured goods, agricultural produce, plastics, glass, energy and all the other products of an industrial economy. But as these tangible essentials are increasingly produced by automated processes, their potential to create value decreases accordingly.

As value is increasingly derived from intangible assets, knowledge and networks, it becomes increasingly difficult to make sense of value creation in conventional terms.

Scarcity and value in cognitive capitalism are often ephemeral and elusive.

My own work could be categorized as *content creation*, but how is this different from content created by software? There are already programs that churn out content based on simple statistics and narratives: Player A scored a goal in the third period, putting Team B ahead, and so on.

If my content is identical to essentially cost-free content created by software, it has very little value.

I think it more accurate to say that I *make sense* of the floodtide of data that wash over us every day.

Someone might code a program that does this as well as I can. When that happens, I will have to do so with more wit and insight than the software or my product will lose its scarcity value.

Should the software's product become wittier and more insightful than my output, I will have to increase a difficult-to-program quality in my work: perhaps it will be *authenticity*, an elusive intangible that humans, with their finely attuned BS detectors, recognize intuitively.

If a sense of humor and whatever other elusive qualities human writers slip into our product get automated, then my work will lose its scarcity value, and I will either have to work for free, beg ("please help support one of the last few human writers of authentic commentary!"), or close up shop.

We can generalize this search for scarcity in a rapidly automating world in this way: those who are most adept at extracting maximum value from machines and software, and then adding what machines and software cannot do on their own, will be scarce.

- Surgeons who extract the most work from robotic surgical tools and then do whatever the robot cannot do on its own will generate the most value.
- Attorneys who extract maximum utility from expert legal software and then bring to bear their courtroom skills or persuasive writing skills will create the most value.

- Software engineers who extract maximum utility from libraries of existing code and automated tools will generate the most value.

Those who do not know how to extract value from the most productive robots and software will not be able to create much value.

This process is not always obvious. Here's an example. We were invited to lunch at our friends' home in Santa Clara a few weeks ago. He's a research scientist at a leading technology company, and she's completing a PhD in computer science.

The husband and I were discussing automation, and I jokingly said that my ability to fix a kitchen faucet is still valuable because programming a robot to perform the troubleshooting, reach under the sink to loosen the fastening nut, and so on would be costly and so it's still cheaper to pay a human to do the repair.

He observed that this would only be true until the faucet was designed specifically to be easily repaired by a robot.

In other words, the architect who designs a building so it is not only well-designed but easy for robots to build will create the most value.

The designer who makes the faucet easy for robots to repair will have created value that is not easy to price, since the ease of repair will last the lifetime of the product.

Our researcher friend suggested self-driving trucks might complete the long haul routes on their own, and then pull over to pick up a driver for *the last mile* through congested city streets.

Once again, the value of human labor is making best use of automation and then adding whatever the software cannot do—in some cases, simply the reassurance that a human is present and watchful.

What's scarce in this new network–based organizational form is knowing how to extract the most value from commoditized technology. Another way of understanding this is: *what's scarce is the ability to choose what to optimize and how to optimize it.* There are always trade-offs in what is being optimized, and those trade-offs are nuanced and dynamic. These skills are difficult to automate because the inputs are constantly changing and may defy quantification.

Increasingly, the resources needed to be productive are free online. But the skills needed to make best use of this vast trove of free resources are not that easy to acquire.

For example, last month a friend emailed me a software script to automate a tedious archival job I needed done. I couldn't get the script to work (no surprise there, I am not a programmer) so I found a CSS template online and tweaked the code to fit my needs. It didn't optimize the task the script performed, but it optimized other aspects of the project.

I could struggle to learn enough of the script's programming language, or I could optimize some other aspect of the project. That choice depended not just on my existing skillset but on a calculation of the future payoff of the project and the potential value of whatever skills I invested scarce time to learn.

For someone anticipating a future in developing software, learning the programming language would have likely been the higher value choice, even though the payoff from the first project was low. But choosing what to optimize is not necessarily obvious, nor is learning *how* to choose what to optimize.

One of the few things we can say with any confidence is that those who develop skills on levels 3 and 4 of Norman Webb's *Depth of Knowledge* (DOK) spectrum (reasoning, inference, planning and investigation) are more likely to grasp the complexities of choosing what to optimize and how to optimize it most productively.

The four levels are:

DOK 1: recall

DOK 2: applications of skills and concepts

DOK 3: strategic thinking

DOK 4: extended thinking

DOK level 2 is easier to automate. Learning one computer language is not enough to ensure your job won't soon be eaten by software. What's scarce is the ability to absorb new information and learn new skills quickly, flexibility, curiosity, attention to detail, adaptability, trustworthiness, responsiveness, autonomy and inventiveness.

These are the core traits of what I term the *Mobile Creative* class. This class is not necessarily mobile in the sense of moving between geographic locations (though they might be); they are mobile in the sense of moving easily between knowledge bases and skills.

Those with little experience in the trenches of technology may be tempted to think *Mobile Creative* work can create more jobs. But this misses the previous point, that automation and digital tools have eliminated 80% of the costs and labor in one sector after another. The 20% of the work that remains places a premium on a specific set of skills, values and motivations. Even if we train everyone in the work force to have those skills and values, it doesn't mean the jobs that were lost are coming back. Increasing the supply of labor does not automatically increase demand for that labor.

Do the remaining jobs generate enough value to earn a moderately middle-class income? As skills become commoditized or automated, their value plummets and the income of those doing the work drops accordingly.

Limits of the Knowledge Economy and Cognitive Capitalism

What can we conclude about the knowledge economy and cognitive capitalism?

Let's start with a question: is this new economic structure stable enough, predictable enough and profitable enough to provide work for everyone displaced by automation?

I think the answer is clearly no. Not only is the number of jobs limited, so is the number of people with the skills, motivation and personality to thrive in an environment where, in Marx's famous description of capitalism, "everything solid melts into air, and the scarcity value of one's work is constantly shifting."

Those who thrive in this environment must absorb massive inputs of information and identify the useful wheat from the irrelevant chaff. They must enjoy learning new things every day, and feel comfortable with Andy Grove's dictum that *only the paranoid survive*: those who rest on their laurels get eaten by competitors or software.

As consultant Heather McGowan observed, "A worker's value is no longer primarily or exclusively about what she knows but rather the speed at which she can learn and apply—this is a dramatic and unsettling shift for many."

The value being created in cognitive capitalism is often not clear. It might be a second-order effect, or the payoff might come in the future. What is the hourly rate for autonomy and inventiveness? No one can say with any precision, because it depends on the scarcity of the output, i.e. the processes and products being produced.

Robin Chase, co-founder of Zipcar, calls this new organizational model *Peers Inc.,* peers opting to collaborate to create value: "Throughout the last century companies have made money by hoarding stuff: assets, intellectual property, people. In the new collaborative economy, sharing and networking assets, like platforms, car seats and bedrooms, will always deliver more value faster."

It's easy to glorify this new organizational structure, where the value is often in the network, not the traditional hierarchies of corporations and states. But the demanding world of cognitive capitalism is not easy to navigate, and I suspect most people find the insecurity of constantly shifting value undesirable.

I think it is unreasonable to expect everyone to develop the constellation of skills, values and traits needed to thrive in such an insecure world, and it is equally unreasonable to expect those seeking profits in this shifting landscape to pay people secure wages.

In other words, the regulations that govern conventional organizations don't work in the knowledge economy, at least not as originally intended. Many are either irrelevant or crippling.

Summarizing the Knowledge Economy

Let's summarize the knowledge economy:

- Value flows to what's scarce.

- Capital and labor are abundant and therefore have little scarcity value.
- As goods and services are commoditized, they lose scarcity value.
- Information and knowledge are also abundant.
- What's scarce is knowledge that results in new processes, products, services and models.
- Many new ideas don't lead to new products, models, etc.
- The process of finding value in new ideas is inherently risky.
- New ideas that automate/commoditize what has yet to be automated/commoditized generate the largest cost reductions and gains.
- Automation/commoditization reduces costs, profits and jobs.

The conclusion of all this is sobering.

Technology isn't going to create more jobs than it destroys.

In an increasingly competitive world of declining profits and rising costs, it is financial suicide to ignore automation in favor of maintaining business as usual.

The companies generating profits in a rapidly commoditized world will not be able to support guaranteed incomes for tens of millions of displaced workers, and borrowing trillions of dollars to fund a super welfare state is not sustainable or desirable, as rapidly rising debt bankrupts the borrower.

Wishful thinking about technology and guaranteed incomes guarantees failure.

Displaced workers need meaningful, secure work. Giving them enough income to scrape by is not enough, as the poverty of lost purpose, pride and positive social roles robs them of the essentials of human life.

The conventional narrative doesn't state this directly, but the unspoken conclusion is: technology is the source of our problems.

But this seems exactly backwards to me. What if technology isn't the source of the problem? What if technology is simply revealing the systemic flaws in the status quo?

Rather than being the source of the problem, what if technology is the solution?

These are the questions we'll explore in the rest of the book.

Questions That Need To Be Asked

The conventional narrative isn't just full of holes; it's incapable of asking questions that threaten its own coherence.

I previously noted two reasons why:

1. We can't imagine a world different from the one we currently inhabit (i.e. a *failure of imagination*)
2. Asking these questions threatens the status quo.

As a result, asking questions is not only not encouraged, it is suppressed via the usual mechanisms: ridicule, marginalization, and variations of *serious people would never ask such a question*.

There is a reason for this: *serious people are being paid not to ask such questions*. In other words, asking such questions could get you demoted, fired or shipped to the bureaucratic equivalent of Siberia.

Here's a question that needs asking: does money have to be created at the top of the pyramid of wealth and power? Put another way: why is the monopoly on creating money reserved for those at the top of the wealth/power pyramid?

Those who claim there is no other way to create money are wrong; technology now enables the *decentralized creation of crypto-currency money*. Money does not need to be created by banks.

Here's another related question: does money have to be borrowed into existence, i.e. the way money is created by banks?

The answer is no, money can now be created digitally and distributed via decentralized networks. It does not have to be borrowed into existence at the top of the pyramid. We will discuss this further in Section Two.

Let's ask another question: is there any connection between money creation and job creation?

The conventional narrative says, yes: money is borrowed into existence to build factories, shops, etc. that employ people.

But borrowing/creating money is not intrinsically connected to creating jobs. Consider the following:

- Let's say I borrow money into existence (i.e. I borrow money from a bank) and use it to buy an apartment building. I raise the rents 20% and immediately start profiting from borrowing the money. But this purchase did not create any new jobs.
- Suppose I borrow money and use it to buy back shares in my corporation. This reduces the number of shares outstanding and boosts the price per share, enriching my holdings of stock while creating no jobs.
- If I borrow money and use it to set up software that automates much of the work being done by my employees, the new money actually eliminates jobs.

These examples are not made up; these are precisely what wealthy individuals and corporations are doing with money created by central and private banks: snapping up income–producing assets, buying back shares and slashing payroll by investing in labor-saving automation.

Each of these increases the wealth of the borrowers without creating any jobs whatsoever.

So in the current way we create and distribute money, there is no intrinsic connection between money creation and job creation. This system of money creation/distribution actually accelerates the concentration of wealth and the destruction of jobs.

This raises another question that is never asked: what if money was created by labor? What if the way to create more money was to do more work? In such a system, money creation would be intrinsically linked to the creation of goods and services. New money would flow to those creating goods and services, i.e. those at the bottom of the wealth/power pyramid rather than at the top.

Money would not be borrowed into existence, so there would be no interest due. Banks would have no role in the creation or distribution of this money. Rather than fuel speculation by already-wealthy individuals and corporations, *this new money would flow to those actually improving the world.*

Here's yet another question: what happens when money is borrowed into existence by banks?

Since the new money is borrowed, it is only distributed to those with substantial income and assets (collateral) to support the new debt—in other words, those who are already wealthy. Those who aren't already wealthy are charged a high rate of interest that effectively transfers a large chunk of their income to the banks.

In other words, borrowing money into existence benefits the banks and the already-wealthy. It siphons income from those with limited incomes and transfers it to the top of the pyramid.

The net result of borrowing money into existence and distributing it at the top of the wealth pyramid is rising inequality. Though apologists (i.e. serious people paid to support the conventional narrative) will claim otherwise, *rising income/wealth inequality is the only possible output of the current financial system.* Given the design and inputs of the system, there are no other possible outputs other than concentrating wealth and power and rising inequality.

Here's another question: what is work?

The typical answer is: labor paid to complete tasks.

But is that really the sum total of what work is? Or is there more to work that getting paid to complete tasks?

What if instead we define work as *creating value*? That raises another question: just how do we assess value?

The conventional narrative answers: work that generates profit has value. The problem with this definition is work can be valuable but not profitable.

Consider the construction of a bikeway—a pathway reserved for bicycles. The project has self-evident value, as bike-only lanes reduce collisions with autos, promote better health by encouraging bicycling and reduces vehicular traffic congestion as people use bicycles instead of autos for some trips.

But none of these indirect benefits is profitable. A profit-maximizing enterprise could only justify building a bikeway if the bikeway generated direct revenue by charging bicyclists to use it. While this is one way to generate profits, it defeats one of the main purposes of the bikeway, which is to encourage safe bicycling for the entire populace, not just those who can afford to pay a fee.

What if we define *creating value* as *meeting the needs of the community*? This covers profitable and unprofitable work: some of the needs can be filled by profit-maximizing enterprises, while others are intrinsically unprofitable. This definition of value opens the door to an entire range of work that creates value without being profitable.

Let's ask a question that no serious person would dare ask: why isn't conventional work more fun?

Since many tasks are not inherently fun in the same way a beach party is fun, let's rephrase the question: what makes people want to go to work, even if the tasks are difficult or unpleasant?

There is no one answer, so let's list a few of the main motivations not directly related to the obvious (and important) one of earning money:

- The person feels needed at work
- The person performs work that is valued
- The person has a say in the work being organized and performed
- The person has a stake in the output beyond his/her wage
- The person takes pride in his/her work, and this pride generates self-worth and identity
- The person feels part of a team
- The work advances their career and/or goals
- The work has meaning

If we had to summarize these points, we might say the person *has autonomy, dignity, ownership and a positive social role*. Having a say in one's work is a form of autonomy. Having a stake in the output is a form of ownership. Being valued as a contributor and having one's work valued defines *a positive social role* that provides dignity, identity and self-worth. Being part of a team provides membership and belonging to something larger than oneself. Work that advances one's career and life goals *builds human and social capital.*

What do we mean when we say work has meaning? That it's profitable to the enterprise? That it has value?

There is more to meaningful work than just creating profit or value. Meaningful work is work that offers participation, not just following orders. Meaningful work offers a stake in the output and the opportunity to build capital, which is the foundation of wealth. Meaningful work advances the worker's personal goals. Meaningful work is recognized as valuable in the community because it is meeting the needs of the community.

If we ask why someone wants to go to work, they might not answer "because it's fun," but their desire reflects motivations that are even more compelling than fun.

Maybe the work itself is dirty, tiresome, stressful drudgery. Nobody would call it fun. But all the elements listed above—collaboration, autonomy, camaraderie, being needed, being recognized as doing important work, belonging and pursuing one's goals—these are the essentials of human life.

But work can be even more than all these essentials. It is *the opportunity to contribute, learn and excel.*

The rewards of such a workplace are not replaceable by leisure and conventional amusements. Being paid to do nothing but consume (i.e. guaranteed minimum income) offers none of these opportunities. Being paid to do nothing is a wasteland of behavioral sinks and lost opportunities to gain the essentials of human life.

No serious economist ponders whether work should be meaningful (or dare we say it—fun). That the core of human life doesn't even register in conventional economics reflects the monumental failure not just of economics but of the conventional narrative.

Work that has been stripped of autonomy, ownership and positive social roles is neither meaningful nor fun. Centralized hierarchies strip away autonomy, meaning, ownership and positive social roles because *that is the only possible output of such systems.*

Why do we tolerate meaningless, unrewarding and unfulfilling work?

For this reason: paid work is scarce. We have to take whatever jobs are being offered by profit-maximizing enterprises or the state that depends on those enterprises for its tax revenues.

And why is paid work scarce? Because money is scarce. If every community could create money by producing goods and services that filled local needs regardless of profit, and do so without having to borrow the money into existence from banks, money would not be scarce. Then paid work would not be scarce, either, because the community could pay everyone fulfilling the community's needs, i.e. those actually improving the world.

If the system that generated the money required decentralized, democratized workplaces and freedom of movement between workplaces, that system's only possible output would be the features listed above that make work meaningful, rewarding and, dare I say it again—*fun*.

The Future Belongs to Work That Is Meaningful

There may be a perfect word for everything beyond a wage that makes people want to come to work, but I confess I can't find it. I have described the elements of work that is purposeful, meaningful and fulfilling: autonomy, ownership, positive social roles, building capital, opportunities to contribute, learn and excel. Condensing this to *meaningful work* expresses our profound need for purpose, pride, dignity, belonging, contributing, participating, collaborating and learning, but it still doesn't capture the joys of work.

In the conventional narrative, work and fun are mutually exclusive. Work is onerous, difficult, boring, unpleasant, and stressful, while fun is partying, shopping, playing games and being entertained.

Saying that work should be fun makes a mockery of its difficulties, and trivializes its many rewards. But discussing work without discussing its potential for joy is to miss an important part of what could and should be.

As an experiment, let's list features of work that are rewarding and even enjoyable, and those that are not.

51

FUN:	NOT FUN
Being productive	Being unproductive
Work with purpose	Work without purpose
Work organized so employees are productive and fulfilled	Work organized to impose hierarchy and control
Autonomy and collaboration	Passively taking orders
Having a say	Having no say
Being threatened with a loss of your livelihood	Being able to choose a different employer/work
Having control of your work	Doing work over which you have no control

I'm sure you get the idea!

In a system in which paid work is abundant, the future belongs to work that is meaningful, and at times, yes, fun, if we define fun as *everything beyond money that makes a person want to go to work.*

These dynamics are often not immediately visible, even to those doing the work.

A recent account (on hardscrabblefarmer.com) about a young man's summer job on a farm expresses this quality of meaningful work. The young man had spent months driving hundreds of cedar fence posts with a sledgehammer. Few would describe this work as fun; most would describe it as hard, tiring, boring, and so on.

The young man had gone on to college, and recently returned to tell the farmer that the days he'd spent working on the farm were some of the best days of his life, and that he'd come to understand their importance in his life.

To those of us with similar experiences, the reasons why the young man valued this work experience so highly are self-evident: he had done good work that was sincerely appreciated. The work had been hard and repetitive but it was purposeful and something he could be proud of.

He could see and touch the results of his work. He hadn't learned a trade so much as learned the value of meaningful work.

A system that doesn't offer this opportunity to everyone is a failed system. Paying people to do nothing but while away their lives as passive consumers is a failed system.

In Section Two, I lay out a system that offers meaningful paid work for all who want it.

Money Creation/Distribution Is Integral to Meaningful Work and Widespread Wealth Creation

The point of all these questions is now clear: the way that money is created and distributed is absolutely integral to the creation of meaningful work and broad-based wealth creation, i.e. *ownership of the output* and *creating human and social capital*.

In the conventional narrative, the creation and distribution of money is completely separate from the creation of jobs and work. Rather than aid widespread wealth creation, the current system of money creation actively widens wealth and income disparity because *this is the only possible output of the system.*

It's clear that the way we create and distribute money is key to generating an abundance of work that meets the needs of the larger community.

In Section Two, I sketch out a system whose only possible output is an abundance of paid work that encourages autonomy, meaning, ownership and positive social roles rather than stripping them away.

But before we can take that step, we need to understand systems, and why their design and inputs dictate their outputs.

Chapter Two: A Quick Lesson in Systems, Hierarchy and Networks

In Chapter One, we analyzed the conventional narrative of automation, technology, jobs and growth and found that:

- Automation does not create more jobs than it destroys.
- A guaranteed income for all is neither practical nor productive.
- Growth is not a sustainable or positive model.

In effect, the conventional narrative has no solutions to automation or poverty—two aspects of the same problem (i.e. the lack of secure jobs). Not only does it have no solutions, it has no concept of any system beyond profit-maximizing corporations and the central bank/state.

Not only has the conventional narrative failed, it is incapable of recognizing its failure. It is equally incapable of recognizing that the current arrangement is impossible to reform because its flaws are intrinsic to its design: it's not the regulations that are flawed, it's the entire structure that's flawed.

- There is no room in this narrative for the possibility that the only systemic solution is a new organizational type that is antithetical to the core characteristics of corporations, banks and the state, i.e. centralization and hierarchy.
- There is no room in the narrative for the possibility that centralization and hierarchy are the problem.

The conventional narrative implicitly assumes there are three structures in the economy: central banks that issue and distribute money and set monetary policy, profit-maximizing enterprises, and the central state that manages the economy. The idea that these structures are not just incapable of solving the problems of automation and poverty but *are the source of the problems*, is inconceivable in the conventional narrative.

The fundamental assumption is that these three are *natural structures* like water, earth and air and that their existence is the natural order. The idea that they are artificial constructs that optimize the interests of the few at the expense of the many is inconceivable.

To expect the current system to generate opportunity, secure work and ownership of the sources of prosperity is the same as expecting a diet of jelly beans and a life of slouching on the couch to generate health.

If we want opportunity, autonomy, secure work and ownership of the sources of prosperity, we need a new system.

The Author's Dilemma: A Thick Doorstop of a Book, or a Summary?

Every author of a book that covers as much ground as this one faces a dilemma: do I explain everything in detail and anticipate every criticism, and end up with a thick doorstop of a book, or do I summarize to keep the book at a reasonable length?

In my case, it's even worse. Every one of the five chapters in Section 1 deserves its own book. As for Section 2—it deserves a doorstop, too.

Rather than write a shelf of books that few will have the time or energy to read, I've opted for a summary that glides over enormous fields of knowledge at a low enough altitude that we get the lay of the land but not every detail.

This demands a lot of you, the reader. For not only is the summary of so many fields a challenge, the analysis upends just about everything we've been told is true about our socio-economic system.

That can be tough to chew and swallow.

So what's the payoff? If we don't understand systems, we can't understand why the current world system is failing, not as some sort of bad luck or storm that will pass but as the inevitable consequence of its design.

And if we can't understand why the current system has failed, we can't design an alternative system that avoids the failure of the present arrangement.

Here's the thing about systems: *changing the participants changes nothing*. People will respond to the incentives presented in much the same way that players of a game respond to the rules. Everybody wants to win, and will play to win based on the rules of the game.

As we have seen, changing the color of the jelly beans (adding regulations, etc.) also changes nothing.

If we want to change the system (or design a new one from scratch), we need to change the rules, processes and inputs. Only then can we get a better result.

What are Systems?

A systems is basically a set of rules-based procedures that process selected inputs and produce outputs. Once you define the processes and the inputs, you've designed a system that can only produce a specific range of outputs.

To change the outputs, you must change the inputs and/or the processes. Alternatively, the other way to change a system is to add a new feedback loop (as explained by Donella Meadows in her work on *leverage points*).

Systems analysis is a huge field, and a few paragraphs can't summarize such a big topic. The point here is that systems analysis enables us to understand complex systems by identifying the basic rules, procedures and inputs.

Let's take a vegetable garden as an example. We could manage the garden in an unsystematic way, following no rules or procedures and not tracking inputs. We could toss whatever seeds we scrounge up on the ground, water whenever we remembered to do so, and not worry about compost or fertilizer.

We might succeed, but most likely our garden will fail to produce the desired output (vegetables) because we didn't provide what the plants needed to thrive.

Alternatively, we set up rules and procedures for planting and maintaining the garden, and carefully track the inputs of seeds, water, compost and fertilizer. Instead of a random toss of seeds, we follow rules on spacing the seeds, putting plants that fix nitrogen in the soil next to plants that need nitrogen, and so on. We set up procedures for watering the garden every third day, and applying compost every week. Every fourth day, we pull up weeds that are competing with our vegetables for nutrients and sunlight.

In a laboratory setting, we are likely to get good results from this system.

But in Nature, random things happen. It might rain very heavily for a few days, damaging the seedlings, or harming the roots of plants that don't like being waterlogged.

If we don't have any feedback in our system, we'll go out in the rainstorm on the third day and drown our plants because the procedures called for watering the garden every three days.

To rectify this, we add a feedback loop: a moisture gauge that tells us when the soil is saturated and when it is dry.

With this new feedback loop of information, we can add a procedure: instead of watering every three days, we'll check the moisture gauge every three days. If the soil is dry, then we'll water. If it's damp, we won't water. If it's somewhat dry, we'll adjust our watering accordingly.

Once we understand the garden as a system, we can see how it could be automated. We could program a robot (let's call it R2Green2) to check the moisture gauge and turn on the drip irrigation system in response to the feedback from the gauge.

We can improve the yields from our garden by collecting data and experimenting with our procedures. For example, we might add composted coffee grounds to one section, or try a different mix of vegetables in one row. By collecting data on what works and doesn't work, we can improve yields. This data is another source of feedback.

Feedback is a key mechanism of systems. Feedback can reinforce itself (positive feedback) or limit the system (negative feedback).

A vehicle's cruise control is an example of negative feedback. Once the speedometer reading exceeds the set speed, the system reduces engine RPMs so the speed drops back into the desired range.

A stock market crash is an example of positive feedback. As the price of stocks drops, some investors decide to sell, either to secure their profits or out of fear that the price could fall further. This selling pushes prices lower, which then triggers more selling, which further depresses prices. Selling triggers more selling, reinforcing the sell-off.

Systems can be *tightly bound* or *loosely bound*. In tightly bound systems, a failure in one part of the system quickly cascades through the rest of the system. In loosely bound systems, failure in one subsystem generates feedback but doesn't cause the entire system to fail.

Tightly bound systems are like intersecting circles of dominoes: if one domino falls, the impact quickly spreads to every circle and eventually topples all the dominoes. Loosely bound systems are like dominoes arranged in independent circles. The collapse of one circle of dominoes does not topple all the dominoes.

If we plant only one vegetable in our garden, we have a *monoculture*. An insect infestation in that one vegetable will wipe out our entire garden. If we have a dozen different kinds of vegetables, the infestation that destroys one type will not wipe out the entire garden.

The more independent (i.e. loosely bound) elements there are in a system, the greater the system's resilience. It may suffer reduced yields due to one crop failure, but the whole garden won't be destroyed.

Systems made of independent elements (what we might call *peers*, since each is equal) are *decentralized*, as opposed to a *hierarchy* in which one element sits at the top of the pyramid and gives orders to all the elements below.

A *peer-to-peer system* is decentralized. We can say these systems are *non-hierarchical*, as the power to make decisions rests with each peer rather than in a hierarchical chain of command.

Non-hierarchical systems *self-organize*, i.e. the participants organize themselves according to the rules of the system. They don't need to be told what to do by a higher authority; they only need to know the rules of the system.

If we combine these concepts, we understand that hierarchies are *tightly bound systems*. A command from the top ripples through the entire system just like dominoes falling. Power and control are centralized rather than *distributed throughout the system*. Alternatively, if information, power and control are in the hands of every peer, this creates a *decentralized, distributed system* that is *loosely bound*. Each peer may receive information from other peers, but no one is forced to follow the same path.

Each peer is a *node in a network* that shares information with every other peer. This structure enables multiple channels of communication and feedback, as opposed to a hierarchical pyramid, in which information only travels in narrow channels up and down the pyramid.

Incentives and Disincentives

A system's rules establish incentives and disincentives. The actual incentives can differ from the incentives intended by the system's designers.

A classic example of this is the Prohibition of alcohol in the U.S. from 1920 to 1933. Well-meaning reformers expected men who had chosen to drink whiskey to meekly switch to drinking milk. Alas, this naïve expectation was spectacularly misplaced, as alcohol consumption went underground, fueling the rise of organized crime.

Though the disincentives against making alcohol were intended to eliminate the scourges of alcohol abuse, Prohibition created enormous financial incentives to smuggle, make and distribute alcohol. The intended results failed to materialize because people responded to the incentives that were actually present, not the well-intentioned but magical-thinking notions of the law's boosters.

Systems *optimize specific strategies and behaviors*: these strategies will yield outsized results while alternative strategies will yield poor results.

Though Prohibition was intended to optimize the elimination of alcohol abuse, it actually optimized the expansion of organized crime and the immensely profitable production and smuggling of alcohol.

Those who followed the rules and stopped making alcohol legally went broke. Those who made or smuggled alcohol illegally reaped fortunes.

The pursuit of self-interest—an entirely predictable dynamic—was *out of alignment with the system's intended goals*. In prohibition, the system's goals were subverted not by a handful of evil individuals but as a result of the system's initial design. In effect, millions of average people were forced into becoming lawbreakers as their self-interest was best served by subverting the system and the rule of law.

By its very design, Prohibition generated *perverse incentives* that undermined the system's goal and the rule of law. The perverse incentives were not limited to alcohol consumption. Law enforcement, taxation, organized crime and the social ills created by pushing alcohol consumption underground were all *tightly bound* in the system of Prohibition. As a result, Prohibition was not an isolated failure; it negatively impacted the economy and the entire social order.

We *optimize what we measure*, and so measuring inputs/outputs incorrectly produces destructive results. The proponents of Prohibition counted the number of breweries, distilleries, bars and taverns closed and deemed Prohibition a great success. They did not count the illegal breweries and distilleries, the kegs of smuggled liquor, the number of bribed law enforcement officials, the swelling profits of organized crime syndicates, the gang wars between syndicates or the deaths caused by wood alcohol.

As these unintended outputs were toted up, proponents of Prohibition were forced to recognize not just the perverse incentives their system had created, but that these perverse incentives were *the only possible output of the system*.

Prohibition was a self-defeating system from its inception. It could not be reformed by passing additional regulations, i.e. changing the color of the jelly beans. The only way to end the mayhem was to end Prohibition.

The Jelly Bean Economy: Self-Interest Is Not Enough

I like jelly beans, and in moderation they're like any other high-sugar, low-nutrition sweet.

But if all we eat is jelly beans, and all we do all day is slouch on a couch, we're going to become ill. If these are the only inputs, ill health is the only possible output. Expecting any other outcome is just wishful thinking.

Let's begin our exploration of self-interest by sketching out a very simple system: the Jelly Bean Economy.

The Jelly Bean Economy has four sectors: the corporation that produces the jelly beans, the state (government) that collects tax revenues from the corporation's profits and payroll, a marginalized sector of people that grow their own fruits and vegetables and don't buy jelly beans, and a pharmaceutical industry devoted to mitigating the ill health caused by a diet of jelly beans.

The implicit goal is this economy is maximizing private gain by whatever means are available.

Jelly Bean, Inc. can only maximize its profits if it sells more jelly beans. To do this, it employs a massive marketing division to sell the notion that every holiday requires a special jelly bean, every life event requires another special jelly bean, and those who fail to buy the latest jelly bean color are uncool, i.e. unworthy of admiration.

Since the all-jelly bean diet is clearly unhealthy, Jelly Bean, Inc. must obscure this negative result with a campaign that masks the consequences of the all-jelly bean lifestyle. Studies that present the negatives are marginalized, ridiculed or countered with intentionally confusing junk-science studies.

The positive aspects of the all-jelly bean lifestyle—the delicious variety of offerings, the fun of shopping for the latest flavors, etc. —are trumpeted as the acme of comfort and enjoyment. A range of products offer the benefits of belonging to jelly-bean based clubs: those who favor red jelly beans have their own club, and so on. Advertisements for the all-jelly bean diet depict slim, attractive people enjoying jelly beans.

The pharmaceutical industry that produces medications to counter the negative health consequences of the all-jelly bean lifestyle is also very profitable. The state collects taxes from this industry and encourages its growth. In effect, good health is unprofitable for the state, since those who grow their own food and don't need medications generate no taxes.

The state, fearful of hurting the profits and payrolls that fund its own taxes, is careful not to hurt sales of Jelly Bean, Inc. or the pharmaceutical industry. The managers of Jelly Bean, Inc. and the pharmaceutical companies encourage this by lobbying state officials and making hefty campaign donations to elected officials (i.e. vote-buying).

One goal of the lobbying is to restrict competition by imposing regulatory barriers to new manufacturers of jelly beans and pharmaceuticals. (This is known as *regulatory capture*.)

The people who grow their own food and refuse to buy jelly beans generate no taxes for the state, so the state best serves its own interests by restricting activities that don't generate taxes. As a result, the state bans urban gardens and restricts the sale of homegrown food.

The participants in each sector are maximizing their private gains: the owners and managers of Jelly Bean, Inc. and the pharmaceutical industry act to maximize sales and profits, and those who work for the state maximize tax revenues by protecting the profits of the sectors that generate the tax revenues.

But the cost of maintaining the system is a population in a permanent state of ill health. Eventually, the costs of this ill health cause the system to fail, as the profits from selling jelly beans and medications no longer cover the costs of ill health.

You may think this example is absurd, but this is more or less how the global tobacco industry operates.

What are the lessons here?

- A system based on maximizing private gain can destroy itself, even as each participant acts out of rational self-interest.
- *Maximizing private gain does not automatically make a system self-sustaining.* The system must be specifically designed so that participants pursuing self-interest strengthen the system rather than weaken it. This may seem obvious, but as we shall see (and as you probably discerned in the Jelly Bean Economy example), the current system is undermined as participants maximize their private gain.
- *In self-defeating systems, maximizing private gain requires obscuring or distorting the truth.* When revealing the truth diminishes one's private gain, self-interest is best served by hiding the truth. In a self-defeating system, those who tell the truth are punished. Those who distort the truth reap the biggest gains.

- A system filled with distorted information can only yield ill-informed decisions and mal-investments. The only possible result of ill-informed decisions and mal-investment is systemic failure.

Half-Truths Generate Incoherence, Distrust and Complexity

When half-truths are issued as fact, the distortions generate incoherence: the narratives based on half-truths no longer make sense when on-the-ground reality is at odds with the half-truths.

This mismatch between official narratives and on-the-ground realities characterizes totalitarian regimes such as the former USSR, where jokes such as "we pretend to work and they pretend to pay us" expressed the gulf between the official narrative and reality.

Maintaining half-truths requires more energy than simply telling the truth, and separating distortions from accurate information also takes more energy. This added complexity—for those issuing the half-truths and those attempting to separate fact from distortion—saps the system of energy that could have been invested productively.

1. All this complexity acts as friction in the system, weakening productivity. Systems that depend on distorted information are stagnant and prone to rising inequality, as the few with access to unadulterated information prosper at the expense of those fed distorted information.
2. A profoundly dysfunctional psychological state arises when participants are denied accurate information. Being constantly bombarded with distorted information generates alienation as the gap between the experience of participants and what they're told is real widens.

In our jelly bean economy example, customers are told the all-Jelly Bean diet is cool, fun and no threat to their health, even as they feel increasingly ill. Eventually this disconnect erodes trust in the companies, the state and ultimately, the entire social order.

Protecting Privilege Causes Systems to Self-Destruct

In Chapter One, I noted that Gilder's *Information Theory of Capitalism* holds that a free-market economy is fundamentally a system that rewards learning and knowledge. In this view, money is a form of information. When a customer buys a product, that exchange of money provides the seller with information.

But when central banks issue new money, the money isn't flowing to new knowledge but to *privilege*. Systems that protect privilege distort information to do so. As noted above, systems that distort information self-destruct.

Therefore, *systems that protect privilege self-destruct.*

To understand the difference between systems that self-destruct and those that are sustainable, let's compare the characteristics of centralized hierarchies and network-based organizations.

Comparing Centralized Hierarchies and Network Organizations

The purpose of centralized hierarchies is control. In other words, *centralized hierarchies optimize top-down power and control.*

The purpose of networks is to distribute knowledge, collaboration and choice. *Networks optimize transparency, shared information and bottom-up collaboration.*

Here is a list of the key characteristics of each organizational type.

Characteristics of Centralized Hierarchies:	Characteristics of Network Organizations:
<ul><li>Control</li><li>Hierarchy</li><li>Centralization</li><li>Authority</li><li>Enforcement</li><li>Obedience</li><li>Commands</li><li>Monopoly</li><li>Avarice</li></ul>	<ul><li>Liberty</li><li>Self-organization</li><li>Decentralization</li><li>Distributed power</li><li>Membership</li><li>Voluntary consensus</li><li>Opt-in/Opt-out collaboration</li><li>Competition/cooperation</li><li>Self-interest</li></ul>

• Concentrated Wealth • Dependence • Secrecy • Scarcity • Exclusivity • Rigid Stability • Fragility • Limited Choice • Atomization • Complicity/Co-option • Learning what you're told to learn • Propaganda • Consumerism • Debt • Fear • Artifice/pretense • Central Planning • Wealth buys political influence • Subservience • Limited social mobility • Privilege	• Distributed knowledge, tools, capital • Self-reliance • Transparency • Abundance • Openness • Flexible stability • Resilience • Diversity • Community • Independence • Self-guided learning • Competing narratives, skepticism • Pursuit of value • Decentralized crypto-currencies • Confidence • Authenticity • Self-organizing enterprises • Participatory democracy • Autonomy • High social mobility • Access

These attributes are native to each system. They are not random, nor can they be transferred from one list to the other. Each list is the *only possible output of each system.*

How Systems Incentivize Self-Destructive Behavior

Why do systems generate perverse incentives that undermine the system itself? Why do participants pursue strategies that lead to the failure of the system itself? Why don't they recognize the self-destructive results of their behaviors?

To answer, we must start with self-interest and incentives in a world of scarcity.

Those who work for organizations that protect the privileges of insiders have enormous incentives to:

- Hide any evidence that their organization is failing to produce the expected results.
- Generate the illusion of success via falsified data, pretense and propaganda.
- Ensure whatever problem the organization was created to address remains unsolved.
- Mask the benefits secured by insiders and exaggerate the benefits the organization delivers to outsiders.

If the system is recognized as a failure, insiders' lucrative employment might vanish. If the problem the system was designed to address is resolved, the system's reason to exist vanishes.

If outsiders discover that insiders are benefiting far more than the intended recipients, pressure to reduce the insider's share will rise. Insiders have a powerful incentive to hide the true scale of their benefits from view.

As a result, every system that offers secure, lucrative work in a world in which such work is scarce is designed by default to institutionalize perverse incentives that undermine the system.

If answered honestly, the question *cui bono*—to whose benefit?—helps identify who's actually benefiting. Insiders will naturally seek to discount their own gain and exaggerate the benefits delivered to outsiders.

In a world of scarcity, insiders draw sharp lines between those who threaten their benefits—outsiders—and those who share the same perverse incentives to mask failure and exaggerate success.

If the organization can suppress all information except carefully scripted PR, outsiders have no means to threaten the insiders' privileges or question their failures.

Organizations that offer secure employment and generate incentives to protect insiders' privileges are called *bureaucracies*. Bureaucracies are *centralized hierarchies*. The only possible outputs of such systems are distorted information and institutionalized failure.

Bureaucracies *optimize the protection of privilege and the suppression of information*. They are thus *self-defeating systems*.

Let's Design Two Work Games

One way to understand systems is to design *a game that has the same rules as the system*. Economists use *game theory* simulations to better understand how the economy works.

We've covered the basics of systems, how the rules of a system optimize certain strategies and incentives, how these can be very different from what the system designers intended, and how maximizing private gain (i.e. pursuing self-interest) can destroy the system from within.

Here are the rules of Work Game #1:

1. You get points for days you show up, not for how much you produce (your output).
2. Producing output costs you points for effort-diligence expended.
3. Your pay (points) go up every year regardless of your output.
4. You can't be fired for low output, only for zero output.
5. It doesn't matter whether your collaborators are productive or not; your pay remains the same.
6. There are only two ways to get more points: either advance to a supervisory position, with 10% more pay and 50% more effort-diligence, or reduce your effort-diligence.

What do these rules optimize? The only possible result of these rules is workers who produce minimal output, since they're not paid for output and producing low output has no penalties.

These are the rules of bureaucracies.

The destruction of positive incentives to produce output was not the intended goal. The goal of those who designed the bureaucracy was to provide job security to all workers, regardless of their output. This laudable goal generates the perverse incentive to do as little as possible. This is what the system optimizes. *There is no other possible output of this system.*

Here are the rules of Work Game #2:

1. Your points are based entirely on your output. Time counts for nothing.
2. The more effort-diligence you invest, the higher your output.
3. The more output your collaborators produce, the more output you produce and the higher your points/pay.
4. Failure to produce high output causes collaborators to shun you, reducing your output.
5. Since there is no hierarchy or boss, you can't be fired. If you do nothing, you earn zero points.
6. There are always abundant opportunities to invest effort-diligence points.

What do these rules optimize? The *only possible result* of these rules is workers who are highly productive, since they're paid only for output and receive nothing for showing up. The penalty for producing nothing is zero points/pay.

There are only two ways to earn more points: either invest more effort-diligence or improve your output so you attract productive collaborators. The rules of this game incentivize productive collaboration, as all collaborators benefit from rising output.

Though points/pay is not guaranteed, the opportunity to earn points/pay is guaranteed.

Work Game #1 models bureaucracies, Work Game #2 models peer-to-peer networks in an environment of *guaranteed work opportunities*. In Work Game #1, pay is guaranteed even if output is minimal. In Work Game #2, pay is near-zero for near-zero output, but there are limitless opportunities to be productive.

Which system is self-destructive, i.e. it creates perverse incentives that undermine the system? Which system sustains itself by aligning the self-interests of players with the sustainability of the system?

These two games reveal a wealth of information about systems, economies and organizations. A productive system guarantees opportunities to generate output and rewards productive collaboration;

a self-destructing system guarantees pay and position regardless of output or collaboration.

The point about games and systems is that all players respond to the same rules and incentives in roughly the same manner because the system optimizes the same behaviors for everyone. Systems don't fail because a handful of individuals are greedy, or succeed because everyone is a saint; they fail or succeed based on what the rules optimize.

The exact same players respond with different behaviors and choices in each of the two games. *Change the system's rules and you change the output. Change the players and you change nothing.*

Let's Design Two Systems for Filling Potholes

Paving degrades with use and time, and as a result there is a constant need to fill potholes in streets and roadways. The conventional state system for filling potholes is a process-heavy bureaucracy:

- A crew surveys a section of streets for potholes.
- Managers gather the data and prioritize which streets get attention first.
- Engineers inspect the high-priority streets and prepare specifications for the pothole-filling.
- The managers prepare a budget for the work and meet with finance department officials to secure funding.
- Plans and specs are drawn up and distributed to private bidders.
- Bids are reviewed and the winning bid chosen.
- The winning bidder submits contractual documents and evidence that he meets all applicable city/state regulations on the composition of his work force, tax compliance, etc.
- The city legal department reviews the contracts and submits revisions.
- The bidder reviews the revisions and negotiates further changes.
- The contract is finally signed by both parties.
- The work is done on street #1. The city inspects the work and the department processes a payment to the contractor.

- The department managers report on progress to city managers, submit an interim financial accounting of projected expenses and request additional funds for cost over-runs.
- The work proceeds street by street until completion.

This system was designed to make all participants accountable to the city's hierarchy, and to record each process so performance can be monitored and audits performed. The productivity of this system is low by design, as productivity was sacrificed to optimize accountability and transparency of procedures.

Let's say the cost in this system is $450 per pothole filled. For wealthy cities that can afford $450 per pothole, this system is accepted as perfectly functional.

But suppose a city can only afford $45 per pothole. If the city adopts the conventional centralized hierarchical system described above, the city can only afford to fill one pothole in ten. The streets will slowly become dangerous as potholes proliferate and vehicles are damaged as potholes get bigger and deeper.

Let's say this city adopted a decentralized, self-organizing system using current technology that retains accountability and transparency but without a costly, slow-moving, low-productivity bureaucracy.

The heart of this system is a queue of bidders and potholes to be filled. The public reports the location and approximate size and depth of potholes on an online database that is visible to everyone. Bidders— which could be everyone from an enterprising fellow with a pickup truck, a work crew organized by a neighborhood or a professional contractor—bid on the job of filling whatever potholes they choose.

The potholes are automatically priced by their location (the busiest streets get the highest priority) and size: the larger, deeper potholes are priced higher than shallow, small potholes.

A large contractor may bid low on an entire street of potholes because he has the crew and equipment to fill dozens of potholes in one day. A neighborhood work crew may bid low on the potholes in their street, just to get them filled as soon as possible. A fellow with a pickup truck may have an open morning and bid low on a couple of potholes just to generate some income rather than be idle.

All of these decisions are made in a self-organizing fashion.

Verifying the pothole has been properly filled is also crowdsourced by citizens. It takes three citizen reports (listing their real names and addresses, which the system cross-checks against public records for accuracy) to confirm the job was done properly. Once the work has been verified, payment is issued.

If a bidder colludes with three citizens to file a false report on a pothole that wasn't filled, this will be readily apparent to anyone who hits the pothole and checks the online work queue. The bidder and the three citizens will be listed on the database as having filed false reports and are immediately banned from the system.

Since the entire system is automated, there are no humans to bribe or threaten. No favors can be granted, no privileges granted or enforced. Anyone breaking the rules is automatically banned from the system. Everyone has skin in the game.

What's hidden from the citizens of the city paying $450 per pothole is the *opportunity cost* of paying $405 more for each pothole that's filled. What else could have been done with that tax money? What more productive uses could that money have been invested in?

In effect, the bureaucracy of filling potholes for $450 each is a *make-work project* for privileged city employees who can't be fired if fewer potholes are filled or the costs rise to $600 per pothole.

As long as the city can raise taxes or borrow more money, the opportunity costs of paying $450 to fill a potholes that could be filled just as effectively for $45 are hidden. But once the city's credit runs out, the opportunity costs will suddenly be painfully visible.

We accept the low-productivity make-work system not because it's faster, better, or cheaper, but because *it's the way things are done* and the inefficiencies, opportunity costs and privileges are enforced by the city's centralized hierarchy.

The Flow of Information in Systems

Information and knowledge are critical to the functioning of systems of every type, from our backyard garden to entire economies. To understand how a system works, we must examine how it handles the flow of information and knowledge.

- Information is more than numerical data; it includes observations and feedback of many types.
- Knowledge is the organization of information into useful fields.

In industrial economies, the flow of materials is a key form of information. For example, the flow of food and firewood into the city and the flow of waste and manufactured goods out of the city is key to understanding the city's economy.

In financial systems, the flow of money, credit and capital are the key forms of information.

In a knowledge economy, the free flow of information and knowledge is the key factor in value creation and productivity.

The only way to increase the wealth of everyone in a system is to increase productivity. If productivity stagnates, wealth creation and social mobility stagnate.

Systems that restrict, hoard or distort the free flow of information shackle productivity. The *only possible outputs of such a system are inequality and instability*, as those with the power to hoard information reap whatever gains are generated while productivity stagnates. These systems are intrinsically unstable, since rising inequality creates imbalances that eventually destabilize the society.

These dynamics are not limited to any one ideology or type of system.

Centralized hierarchies limit, hoard or distort the free flow of information to serve their core function, which is to *preserve the privileges of the few at the expense of the many*. The only way to defend these privileges is to limit information to those at the top of the power pyramid.

If we understand that *money and credit are forms of information* that contain data about risk, value and capital, we understand why money and credit in centralized hierarchies flow to the top of the pyramid.

Limiting the free flow of information necessarily limits productivity.

In other words, you cannot simultaneously have a centralized hierarchy and a free flow of information and knowledge. The two are mutually exclusive. Without a free flow of information and knowledge, you cannot improve productivity in a knowledge economy. It then follows that you cannot have a centralized hierarchy and a highly productive system that broadly distributes gains in productivity.

If we put these together, we conclude that the *only possible outputs of centralized hierarchy are stagnation, inequality and instability*. These characteristics can be masked by productivity-boosting inputs such as cheap energy and credit, but once these temporary inputs decline, the system's outputs revert to stagnation, inequality and instability.

Centralized Hierarchies Optimize Politics and Information Distortion

If we compare the lists of attributes of centralized hierarchies and networks, we notice centralized hierarchies optimize *politics and the hoarding/distorting of information*. In contrast, networks optimize *transparency*, *free flow of information* and *verification* that builds trust.

One way to understand why each system optimizes such different characteristics is to analyze how each system handles the flow of information/knowledge.

Though knowledge is intangible, it is also quite real. Consider the following:

- If citizens are given incorrect information about their government's actions, their consent is prone to collapse once the truth becomes known.
- If market participants are given inaccurate information about a company's earnings, their investment decisions will be prone to catastrophic losses once the truth becomes known.
- If a spouse discovers their mate's infidelity, their life is irrevocably altered by this knowledge.

In centralized hierarchies, information and knowledge are dangerous because they can undermine vested interests. Since those in centralized hierarchies understand knowledge is intrinsically risky, their first priority is controlling information/knowledge to distribute what reflects positively on them and bury everything that is negative. This robs the system of vital information and feedback, disabling the system at the most fundamental level.

The need to control information optimizes public relations (PR) and propaganda, i.e. the engineering of half-truths and falsehoods.

In hierarchies, power is concentrated in the apex of the system. Given the risk of uncontrolled information, the system optimizes *loyalty to superiors* rather than loyalty to the organization's purpose. Advancing a person who places loyalty to the unvarnished truth and dissent above loyalty to his superiors makes no sense in centralized hierarchies. Indeed, such a person is a high-risk threat.

As a result, advancement in centralized hierarchies is necessarily a *political process* of proving loyalty to superiors and displaying mastery of controlling information. These intrinsically political skills are what centralized hierarchies optimize. Fulfilling the organization's mission is secondary to maintaining control of information and securing the loyalty of the chain of command.

In network-based systems that lack hierarchies (or have very flat hierarchies), subverting knowledge puts everyone who has been denied information at a disadvantage. Those who bury information to make themselves look good cripple their collaborators. In such a system, those who withhold information are shunned as toxic risks.

Interestingly, each system optimizes the opposite set of skills.

- Centralized hierarchies optimize politicking—loyalty to superiors and controlling information—attributes which are inherently destructive to participants in distributed network-based systems.
- In distributed network-based systems, loyalty to the free distribution of factual information and knowledge is paramount, as only good information can support trust and informed decision-making.

Systems that optimize untrustworthy information also optimize *flawed decisions* and *the erosion of trust in the system*. As a result, centralized hierarchies optimize defective decision-making and the erosion of trust. It follows that centralized hierarchies undermine democracy, markets and productivity at the most basic level of information flows and trust.

The Disadvantages of Hierarchy

Judging by human history, hierarchies are built into human nature. But this doesn't mean they don't have systemic drawbacks.

Hierarchies concentrate power in the top of the pyramid. To the degree that wealth is simply another manifestation of power, hierarchies concentrate wealth and power in the hands of the few at the top.

Hierarchies optimize control, and centralized capital optimizes economies of scale. Corporations that organize capital and human labor to optimize profits are highly successful because they exploit economies of scale so efficiently.

Hierarchies are fundamentally based on obedience to superiors and the enforcement of commands. This structure creates two systemic disadvantages.

Those in command have leverage over those below because they can deprive them of their pay or position. This leverage can serve the self-interest of those in power rather than the interests of the organization.

Coercion is the core of hierarchy, and those with power face the temptation of using their leverage to optimize their own private gain at the expense of those below.

All hierarchies have mechanisms to limit optimization of private gain at the expense of the organization, but this mechanism contains a built-in in tension that cannot be resolved: those tasked with rooting out the optimization of self-interest are themselves tempted to optimize their private gain.

Hierarchies by necessity limit feedback flowing up to the leadership. The few at the top do not have enough time or expertise to analyze all the feedback. The job of each link in the chain of command is to summarize feedback from below before passing it up the chain. But given that the self-interest of each person in the hierarchy is only served by pleasing their immediate superiors, the default setting is to report only what pleases one's superiors. Those who demand honesty will face the same dilemma when they report to their superiors: will an honest report hurt their own interests?

This accretion of self-interest and fear of disapproval builds as it moves up the pyramid of command. This process can lead to tragic absurdities being taken as truth. In one famous example in Mao-era China, underlings had rice planted in thick abundance along a particular stretch of roadway, so that when Chairman Mao was driven along this roadway, he would see evidence of a spectacular rice harvest.

In reality, China was in the terrible grip of a famine resulting from disastrous state policies. But since everyone feared the consequences of telling Mao his policies were starving millions of Chinese people to death, the highway was planted to mask the dangerous reality.

This narrowing of feedback has other systemic consequences.

Even the most honest reports reflect the biases of those summarizing feedback. As a result, when the feedback finally reaches the top leadership, it may be inaccurate in ways that are difficult to detect. Put another way, dissent has been edited out or perfumed.

All leaders have their own biases and experiential limits, and these have the potential to lead to disastrous decisions.

Networked organizations are exposed to constant feedback, and there is no advantage to editing feedback to please superiors because there isn't a chain of command. Disastrous decisions wipe out a single network node, but in a centralized hierarchy, a disastrous decision can wipe out the entire organization.

This is the weakness of organizational pyramids based on obedience and authority.

To take a military example:

In a traditional army:	In a network of irregulars:
A command for a near-suicidal assault must be obeyed.	Each unit can opt out of the suggestion that such an assault is necessary
Top commander can decide that the enemy's perimeter defense is about to give way and order the direct assault. The frontal attack will result in horrendous losses because there was no feedback to modify the disastrous decision of the commander.	One unit might try to penetrate the perimeter, and be wiped out after an initial success. Nearby units will realize the enemy has changed tactics and has constructed a depth of defense designed to lure in and destroy a direct assault.

In other words, it's not just the quality of the feedback that matters; it's the speed and integrity of the feedback loop that matters.

Consider the incentives presented to participants below the apex of power: their rewards (salary, pension, vacation time, etc.) are set the moment they sign their employment contract. The only way to obtain more rewards is to advance within the power pyramid, which means exaggerating one's loyalty to superiors and optimizing the skills of information hoarding.

The only other way to maximize the rewards of participating in a hierarchy is to *minimize inputs*—work, effort, caring. Unsurprisingly, this is the avenue the least ambitious choose to pursue their self-interest: perform the least amount of work possible, and minimize effort and diligence.

Once again, we find the incentives undermine the effectiveness of the system, as each participant seeks to maximize their personal gain within the hierarchy. Once again, we see that the incentives are out of alignment with the goals of the system.

Despite the disadvantages of their structure, hierarchies offer efficiencies in control and economies of scale. In the industrial revolutions that favored the information of material and money, these benefits outweighed the disadvantages.

But in the digital revolution of the knowledge economy, these disadvantages become fatal.

Many within the corporate and state leadership are acutely aware of this, and are seeking to incorporate the free flow of information, autonomy and inventiveness that are native to networks into their hierarchies.

But it is an open question whether the free flow of information, autonomy and inventiveness that are native to network organizations can be grafted onto hierarchies, given that each of these is incompatible with hierarchy. Ultimately the only way to free hierarchies from their intrinsic limitations is to eliminate the centralized hierarchical structure itself.

Let's look at the subprime mortgage/housing bubble as an infamous example of structural flaws leading to the collapse of the entire system.

The Subprime Mortgage/Housing Bubble and Collapse

Like most catastrophic collapses of apparently stable systems, the seeds of the subprime mortgage/housing bubble were sown with the best intentions.

The leadership of the federal housing agencies wanted more households to benefit from homeownership, so they loosened lending standards to marginal (high-risk) borrowers and rewarded banks for issuing mortgages to these risky borrowers.

At the same time, the elected leadership and top federal financial regulators wanted to free banks to issue more exotic financial instruments (derivatives, credit default swaps, etc.) because experts persuaded them that more financial freedom would lower overall costs by offering more ways to distribute risk.

Mortgages that were once held by lenders for the entire 30-year term were securitized into mortgage-backed securities (MBS)—sliced into tranches, bundled and sold to investors. This innovation enabled the lenders to earn the profits of originating the mortgage upfront and offload the risks of holding the mortgages to others.

Banks lobbied hard for these changes because the freedom to sell more investment-banking services would enable greater profits. Bank lobbying included substantial contributions to the campaigns of elected officials.

The number of people who made these decisions was very small. This was not accidental; this is the nature of highly centralized hierarchies. In each case, the leadership (of banks, Congress and the regulatory agencies) acted not only out of self-interest but also on the advice of experts within their hierarchies.

Very quickly, these top-down changes generated perverse incentives.

The agencies tasked with rating the risk of mortgage-backed securities (MBS) were paid according to the volume of MBS they rated (another example of *we optimize what is measured*). Since issuing high risk ratings might cause lenders to use other ratings agencies, the agencies downplayed various risk factors to ensure robust sales and profits.

Lenders found the global market for highly rated (and highly profitable) MBS was insatiable, and so they lowered risk-management guidelines to encourage mortgage brokers to sell as many mortgages as possible. That is, they changed the input requirements/rules to get the output they wanted.

This led to no-document mortgages, known colloquially as *liar loans* because the borrower did not need to verify income with tax documents, wage stubs, etc.

The loosening of lending standards and the expansion of federally insured mortgages issued by Fannie Mae and the Federal Housing Administration (FHA) expanded the issuance of low down payment mortgages, enabling marginal buyers to qualify for mortgages with as little as 3% down.

This vast expansion of mortgages to marginally qualified buyers expanded home ownership, the desired goal of the policies, and this burnished the reputations of the housing agencies and their leaders.

These policies eventually led to no-document, no down payment, negative-amortization mortgages where unqualified borrowers could buy a home with nothing down and have monthly payments that were lower than the interest due.

This expansion of mortgages to marginally qualified borrowers created a large new pool of homebuyers, and as these buyers bought homes, this increasing demand pushed prices higher. Even as builders rushed to construct more homes to take advantage of soaring demand, prices continued moving higher.

Investors observed this rapid price appreciation and responded by buying homes for speculation. This practice was known as *house-flipping*: an investor bought the home (often when it was still under construction or even in the planning stages) with as little down payment as possible, waited for prices to appreciate and then sold the home for a substantial profit.

This speculative buying further expanded demand which then drove prices higher. This created a *positive feedback loop*—every push higher in prices generated more activity that boosted prices even higher.

What is noteworthy in this feedback loop of mortgage originations, securitization, federal agency participation and stamps of approval by ratings agencies is how each participant was simply optimizing the incentives presented to them by the system. The excesses were not the result of individual wrong-doing (though there were plenty of instances of outright fraud); rather, participants large and small were acting to maximize their own gains by responding rationally to the incentives the system presented.

Those within the mortgage/finance sectors who failed to pursue the incentives to speculate had poor results and were fired. This Darwinian winnowing of the scrupulous and skeptical in favor of those who maximized leverage further fueled the downplaying of risk at the heart of the bubble.

Not only was greed rational in this speculative frenzy, it was seen as positive, because this expansion of risk and speculation was fueling growth—not just in home building, but in tax revenues, mortgage origination and the general economy.

A great many observers (myself included) recognized the dangers of this expansion of risk and speculation, but our warnings were ignored or downplayed.

The inevitable bursting of this risk-speculation-credit bubble collapsed not just the mortgage system but almost collapsed the entire financial ecosystem. As noted earlier, this is a core feature of centralized hierarchies: participants respond to the incentives presented, even if they are perverse and self-destructive to the system itself.

Though few seemed aware of the domino-like risks, mortgages and MBS were *tightly bound* to the entire financial system. The collapse of subprime mortgages knocked down the entire mortgage sector which then very nearly toppled the entire global financial system.

This highlights one exceedingly dangerous characteristic of centralized hierarchies: systems that appear only loosely connected are tightly bound by centralization itself. Loosening lending regulations and enabling the securitization of mortgages did not affect just the mortgage and investment banking sectors; by changing what the entire system optimized, the centralized regulatory hierarchies tightly bound every sector connected to finance, which ultimately included the entire global economy.

The mortgage/housing debacle illustrates every core disadvantage of centralized hierarchies:

- A handful at the top of the hierarchy pyramid made decisions based on good intentions, the advice of experts and their own self-interest.
- The policies incentivized behaviors (rampant risk taking and speculation) that were not aligned with the stated goals of the policies (expanding home ownership to those previously denied ownership due to tight lending standards).
- Since home ownership, home prices, profits and growth all expanded (and since *we optimize what we measure*), the policies were deemed enormously successful until the system collapsed.
- The inputs needed to maintain expansion—more marginal borrowers, more buyers of risky MBS and more speculators—

dried up as everyone who wanted to play was already in the game.

- Insiders rigged the rules (i.e. *gamed the system*) to enable the marketing of high-risk securities and mortgages as low-risk investments. As the bubble expanded, this *information asymmetry* (i.e. only the insiders knew the real risks of the MBS) created a system in which *some were more equal than others*.
- The leadership of the regulatory hierarchies accepted that risk had been lowered throughout the system by exotic financial instruments and chose not to pursue clearly fraudulent activity because doing so would have derailed the positive feedback that was driving growth.

The excesses created by changing the rules could not have occurred in a decentralized system of network nodes that could each set the price of mortgages, risk and homes based on feedback from all the other nodes in the network.

The excesses and the collapse were only possible in a centralized hierarchy.

Indeed, it is clear in hindsight that *collapse was the only possible output of this system*.

This collapse was not unique to the mortgage sector, though apologists will argue that it was a one-off. Rather, the collapse was the direct consequence of the structure of centralized hierarchies.

The core characteristics of centralized hierarchies that led to this systemic collapse include:

- The flow of information was restricted to serve the vested interests at the top of the power pyramid.
- Decisions based on distorted information about risk were disastrous to those who trusted the information.
- When trust in the validity of information about risk eroded, the system crashed.
- Since mortgages, housing, investment banking, exotic financial instruments and the financial system were all tightly bound, the

collapse of the mortgage sector very nearly toppled the entire financial system.

- The participants' pursuit of self-interest (i.e. acting on the incentives presented) undermined the entire system.

No central authority ordered people to game the system, lie on their mortgage applications, exaggerate the safety of mortgage-backed securities or discount the risks; participants optimized their gains according to the rules and incentives presented. Given another set of rules and incentives, they would have made other choices.

When information is distorted or withheld and persuasion is substituted for knowledge, trust is lost and the system collapses. *This is the teleology of centralized hierarchies; there is no other possible output.*

As noted in the section on Work Games: change the system's rules and you change the output. Change the players and you change nothing.

The Failure of Incremental Reform

One of the larger holes in the conventional narrative is the blindness to the impossibility of reforming centralized hierarchies with additional regulations. If we understand centralized hierarchies as tightly bound systems that optimize the restriction of information, loyalty to superiors, and perverse incentives, we understand why 1,000 pages of additional regulations merely reduces whatever latent efficiencies the system might still retain while changing nothing in the structure or the results.

- Requiring people to assure regulators that they are not restricting information merely incentivizes Orwellian doublespeak and limiting information in ways that cannot be documented.
- Requiring participants to claim that their loyalty is to factual reporting and dissent is asking them to sacrifice any hope of advancement within the organization.
- Writing 1,000 pages of arcane regulations to tease apart tightly bound systems merely binds the subsystems even more tightly to the regulatory structure, reinforcing the contagion of failure.

The only way to truly reform centralized hierarchies is to dismantle the structures that make them centralized hierarchies in the first place. Once you remove a hierarchy's ability to restrict and distort information, you've removed its ability to reward its insiders and defend their privileges. With those gone, what's left to sustain the organization?

At this point, we have to ask: what's the advantage of maintaining centralized hierarchies in the first place?

The Historical Context of the Current World System

Systems arise to optimize a particular historical context of resources, labor and capital. In doing so, they make trade-offs. When conditions change, those trade-offs are no longer productive and the system becomes self-destructive.

In broad brush, the first and second Industrial Revolutions optimized the movement and processing of materials because these were the sources of value creation. In terms of information theory, the information/knowledge needed to assemble and process materials—from shipping raw ore to make steel that is fashioned into vehicles, tools, buildings, etc.—was the source of profits and hence what would naturally be optimized.

Thus it is no surprise that early in the 20th century the Ford Motor Company optimized vertical integration of its entire supply chain, from making steel to fabricating the vehicles, or that Walmart optimized the *just in time* supply chain from Asian manufacturers to its stores around the globe in the 1990s.

But as production of goods and the optimization of the supply chain are both being commoditized by software and robotics, these are no longer the engines of value creation.

The information/knowledge needed to create and sell exotic financial instruments—the engine of value creation we call *financialization*—is also being commoditized by software.

Both industrialization and financialization thrive on information hoarding and exploiting asymmetrical information, i.e. maximizing profits by exploiting what only insiders know.

As industry and finance are commoditized, the pay-off from hoarding information declines. As information is digitized, *everyone has access to the same information*. This lowers the value of hoarded information.

Here's an example from everyday life. In the 1960s, the U.S. spent billions of dollars developing sophisticated spy satellites that could take sharp photos of the Earth's surface from low-Earth orbit. The technology of capturing and transmitting these images was one of America's most closely guarded secrets.

This information was highly asymmetric. Only the very top echelons of America's national security agencies had access to these photos. There was no replacement for this imagery; its national-security value was unique.

Now, anyone with a digital device can view a Google Earth image with about the same resolution as the 1960s top-secret spy satellites. Information that was once highly valuable and closely guarded is now available to everyone.

As a result, enterprises are making use of these images in new and productive ways. Space-based imagery is helping to improve crop yields (by noting the color of fields) and information on production (counting new vehicles stored on parking lots).

In the first and second Industrial Revolutions, information and knowledge about materials and supply chains were hoarded as competitive advantages.

In the knowledge economy, hoarding information and knowledge about processes undergoing rapid commodification is a one-way ticket to the graveyard. While basic patents may still demand a premium, value is created by innovating and adapting faster than competitors, not by hoarding information.

Value is created by sharing knowledge with collaborators, not hoarding knowledge.

The processes centralized hierarchies and bureaucracies optimize are no longer engines of value creation. As their costs outweigh the value they create, these structures are self-destructing.

Just as profit-maximizing corporations optimized the production of goods and global supply chains, central states optimized control of vast departments and sprawling national projects with bureaucracies.

In the world of slow paper communications and low productivity, bureaucracies optimized reliability and management of complex systems such as armies and navies.

Even in a world revolutionized by radio, the vast industries and military forces of World War II were managed largely with paper orders and invoices. (In the mid-1950s, my father's paystubs from the nation's largest retailer, Sears Roebuck & Co., were still hand-written by a clerk; he received a carbon-paper copy.)

Of the 400,000 females who served in the U.S. Armed Forces in World War II, roughly 70% performed office work as clerks, typists, etc. This vast army was augmented by another army of male clerks, typists, etc.

Since wages and benefits were modest, these systems could afford redundancy and multiple layers of management that offered a measure of cumbersome but generally effective reliability.

But for all the reasons covered in Chapter One, wages and benefits rise inexorably, and bureaucracies are now high-cost systems. These systems' low productivity is now a cost borne by the many to benefit the few.

Systems that optimized the movement of materials and financialization also optimized the expansion of consumption and debt, i.e. growth. If growth of consumption and debt are no longer possible due to resource limits and over-indebtedness, these systems collapse as costs rise and profits disappear.

Simply put, we need a new system that optimizes value creation in the knowledge economy, and that optimizes a low-debt economy that does more with less, what we call *Degrowth*. The old centralized hierarchies and bureaucracies are doomed, no matter how many reforms and regulations are imposed by those seeking to protect their privileges. These added costs and complexities are only greasing the current world-system's slide to the graveyard.

Chapter Three: Scarcity, Productivity and Privilege

We are now in a position to understand how productivity, profits, privilege, commoditization, money creation, democracy, inequality and instability are connected systemically.

Once again, I remind you that by all rights you should be opening a whole new book here, as each topic is an entire landscape in itself. But since we're going to design a whole new system in Section 2, we need to keep summarizing lest we end up with a pile of doorstop books.

This is a lot of connections to make, so let's summarize what we've found so far:

The *only possible outputs of centralized hierarchy in a knowledge economy are stagnation, inequality and instability*.

Centralized hierarchies protects the privileges of the few at the expense of the many.

Protecting privilege is incompatible with innovation, since innovation inevitably threatens the structures that protect privilege. As a result, systems optimized to protect privilege inevitably stagnate as the costs of protecting the privileged rise while productivity suffers.

It's a simple choice: either we choose to protect centralized hierarchies and accept stagnating productivity, or you choose decentralized, self-organizing innovation and high productivity. You can't have both.

Just as stagnating productivity impoverishes everyone, rising productivity and the *faster, better, cheaper* of innovation benefits everyone.

The current world system is not just an economic order; its structure also generates a political and social order which is as self-destructive as its economic structure.

Artificial Scarcity and Stagnation

In earlier chapters, we found that value flows to scarcity. In a transparent market, scarce goods and services will command higher prices and generate higher profits.

We also found that when goods and services are commoditized by automation, their scarcity value plummets, along with profits.

Privilege works by enforcing an artificial scarcity on accurate information. The few with access to accurate information skim the gains from scarcity not by improving productivity or producing scarce goods and services, but by exploiting the *artificial scarcity* enforced by centralized hierarchies such as states, central banks and monopolies.

Overall wealth is not increased by this exploitation of artificial scarcity. Rather, this concentration of gains into the hands of the privileged few who produce no value—no new goods or services or innovations—robs the system of capital that could have fueled improved productivity.

The opportunity cost of maintaining the privileges of the few via artificial scarcity are immense, as productive uses for the capital diverted to the privileged few go begging.

Artificial scarcity enforced by centralized hierarchies has *only one set of possible outputs*: increasing stagnation, inequality and instability.

What Efficiencies Do Centralized Hierarchies Optimize?

Much is made of the efficiencies enabled by centralized hierarchies: economies of scale and mass concentrations of capital, labor and talent. These efficiencies bore fruit in the first and second Industrial Revolutions, which were dominated by manufacturing and advances in supply chain integration. Those few able to concentrate capital, labor and expertise in a factory reaped enormous gains as integrated supply chains lowered costs and mass production ramped up output.

In the knowledge-based economy:

- Manufacturing and supply chain optimization have largely been commoditized, and automation is continuing to commoditize what hasn't already been stripped of scarcity value.

- The economies of scale optimized by centralized hierarchies have been reduced to low-margin, low-profit processes by automation and global competition.
- Scarcity value is optimized by network-based organizations. Those centralized hierarchies that harvest this scarcity value do so only by adopting the features that are native to networks: autonomous working groups, free flow of information within the enterprise, rapid response to changing markets, etc.

In general, centralized hierarchies that optimize commoditization are low profit margin businesses that are highly exposed to global competition and the impact of automation. The only way conventional centralized hierarchies can reap outsized profits is if they create a monopoly—either one that is enforced by the state via regulations or by becoming the dominant provider in a sector.

If you are tempted to list Apple, Facebook and Google as evidence that centralized hierarchies are highly profitable, please recall that there is *only one Apple, one Facebook and one Google on the planet*, and that these firms have fewer than 100,000 employees in the U.S. and fewer than 150,000 globally—a negligible slice of America's workforce of 150 million. As detailed earlier, their combined profits are a negligible sliver of what America's state spends every year ($6.2 trillion).

A small handful of global corporations have managed to integrate the features of networks that enable free flow of information, collaboration, and rapid feedback. These few are outliers, not examples of the norm.

And as noted earlier, innovations based on economies of scale are quickly commoditized by competitors. There is no guarantee that even the most enlightened centralized hierarchies will remain profitable unless they secure a monopoly.

Monopoly is the Perfection of Centralized Hierarchy

Monopoly—the destruction of competition and the market's ability to discover price—is the perfection of centralized hierarchies. If given the chance, every centralized hierarchy would instantly choose to become a monopoly, as only monopoly enables gains in a stagnating economy.

Monopoly *optimizes stagnant productivity, high opportunity costs, and the concentration of gains to the privileged few at the expense of the many.* The only possible output of monopoly is reduced competition, productivity and innovation.

Competition is the result of new knowledge entering the system. Competition = innovation.

Innovation that increases productivity and total wealth is suppressed by monopoly. Those with the monopoly have no incentive to risk developing innovations, since the highest return strategy is to bribe the state to enforce their monopoly.

Capital that could have been invested in innovation is diverted to the privileged few. As a result, systems dominated by monopolies stagnate as inequality rises and innovation is stifled.

Monopoly distributes these gains to the few not as a reward for improving productivity but for suppressing competition/innovation.

Productivity requires the free flow of knowledge and information, which manifest as competition and transparency in the marketplace. With knowledge and information stifled, competition and transparency die— and so do productivity, democracy and markets.

The free flow of information that builds trust and rewards new knowledge is the source of productivity. Monopoly destroys all three.

These are all tightly bound: you cannot maintain productivity within monopoly, nor can you sustain a monopoly in a transparent system of free-flowing knowledge.

Monopoly and centralized hierarchies are thus incompatible with any system that need competition and free flow of information to flourish: for example, free markets and democracy.

What's Scarce?

What's scarce as a result of the current system's structure?

In a transparent market, value flows to scarcity. In monopolies, scarcity is artificial. If the company store is the only store in town, what's scarce is competition and consumer choice. The scarcity of competition is entirely artificial—the consequence of the company's monopoly.

In centralized hierarchies, unfiltered information is scarce, and this scarcity generates the value skimmed by the privileged few with access to unfiltered information.

In the financial world, access to cheap capital and the ability to create money is scarce.

In systems that optimize privilege, openings in the ranks of the privileged are scarce. This scarcity is completely artificial, that is, it is created by the structure of the system, not by the workings of a transparent market.

Artificial scarcity generates the high returns on privilege. But as we have seen, enforcing artificial scarcity erodes precisely what systems need to be vibrant, resilient and adaptable: the free flow of information, knowledge and feedback.

Systems of privilege optimize all the dynamics that undermine democracy, opportunity and markets: innovation, competition, choice, informed decisions and rising productivity.

Systems Not Based on Protecting Privilege

In a world dominated by monopolies and centralized hierarchies, the stagnation of productivity and opportunity is predictable because these are the only possible output. The conventional narrative is blind to this, and so the following question never comes up: what does a system that isn't based on maintaining privilege look like?

To answer this, we can start by looking at human life before the rise of centralized hierarchies, back when humanity had been driven by climate change into a narrow strip of South African coast about 160,000 years ago.

There is evidence that this highly stressful environment—scarce resources and competing groups of humans—reinforced our ability to cooperate and to fight, as both strategies proved useful in securing and defending scarce resources. In this competitive environment, small groups cooperating with other groups to defend scarce resources optimized communication, collaboration, sharing of resources and the burdens of defense and a wide spectrum of technical and social innovations.

In such an intensely competitive environment that optimized cooperation, communication and rapid feedback (the location of potential intruders, who is currently defending our resources, etc.), the privilege of leadership would have been indefensible without the consent of the governed, i.e. the membership of each small group.

The privilege of leadership was contingent on the success of the leadership, as everyone in the group had "skin in the game" and would suffer the painful consequences of poor leadership and decisions made on faulty information: hunger, loss of resources and possibly death in combat with stronger, better led competitors.

What was scarce in this environment? Secure sources of food and water, the skills needed to communicate and cooperate with other friendly groups to better defend those resources, access to social and technical innovations, trustworthy information about rival groups and new resources, and so on—in other words, the free flow of trustworthy information and knowledge and multiple rapid-cycle feedback loops.

In such a challenging environment, leadership skills were undoubtedly scarce. The privilege that flowed to this scarcity was contingent on the success of the leadership.

This system optimizes responsive, effective leadership, as whatever privileges are awarded in exchange for the burdens of leadership are contingent on results. It also optimizes fast, productive learning—not just in the leadership, but in the entire membership, for the rapid development and distribution of innovations is best served by a diverse group testing and modifying the innovations in the field.

Dissent is also optimized, as groups that never question their leadership are more likely to suffer the consequences of poor leadership.

If we recall the attributes of network-based organizations, it's clear that these early human groups were decentralized, network organizations that *optimized transparency, active participation, shared information and access to resources and bottom-up collaboration.*

92

Humans adapted to decentralized, network-based systems as a matter of survival. Whatever hierarchies that existed were flat (i.e. only two layers, leaders and members) and contingent on results, not authority.

Contrast this with centralized hierarchies that funnel most of the gains to the privileged few, a system that optimizes perverse incentives, monopoly, stagnation, inequality and instability.

In centralized hierarchies, the key skills are not rapid advancement of knowledge or innovating; the key to advancements are politicking and distorting/hoarding information.

If we add all this up, it's easy to understand why the current world system, dominated by centralized hierarchies and monopolies, is increasingly stagnant and unstable. It's also clear that humans' long history optimized us for just the sort of systems that thrive in the knowledge economy: highly decentralized, adaptable, networked and transparent.

Chapter Four: Centralized Money, Wealth and the Subversion of Democracy

As noted previously, central banks, the state and profit-maximizing enterprises are viewed in the conventional narrative as the equivalents of earth, air and water—natural systems for which there is no alternative.

But each of these is actually a social construct. There is nothing inevitable about them.

It can be argued that government manifests humanity's innate preference for hierarchy and profit-driven enterprises manifest our innate self-interest, but what's the argument for central banks maintaining a monopoly on the issuance and distribution of money?

In previous eras, states stamped coins out of precious metals. But the value of each coin was ultimately based not on promises of the state but on the intrinsic value of the metal that had been fashioned into a unit of money.

In the current system of fiat money, i.e. money that has no intrinsic value, banks create money by issuing loans. This ability to create money by issuing loans based on small reserves of actual cash is called *fractional reserve lending*, because the banks can issue a $20 loan for every $1 of reserve (cash). Put another way, banks only hold $5 of every $100 of assets as actual cash collateral.

This system benefits the few with access to bank credit and the ability to use *fractional reserve lending* to create multiples of cash via issuing credit (loans). This system *concentrates wealth in the hands of the few - whose wealth then subverts democracy.*

This is not an accidental or random feature of centralized money issuance; it is *the only possible output of the system.*

Central banks have a monopoly on issuing and distributing money and credit. Given that monopolies generate stagnation, inequality and instability, and central banks are monopolies *par excellence*, it is unsurprising that the central bank system rewards privilege, not productivity or innovation.

The key feature of the central bank system is that the money/credit is not distributed to those producing goods and services—the *money/credit flow only to the privileged few at the top.* In other words, the creation and distribution of money/credit are completely disconnected from the production of value. The money/credit flow only to the privileged few who can use this credit to buy productive assets, outbidding those who only have savings. With such an advantage, the wealthy few become increasingly wealthy, as they buy up more assets and gain the income from these assets.

No wonder financial inequality is rising; *widening wealth inequality is the only possible output of central banking/fractional reserve lending.* We can understand this by considering the difference between an individual and a bank.

The Monopoly on Money Creation and Rising Wealth Inequality

An individual cannot borrow money directly from the central bank. He must go to a private bank which has access to low-cost funds issued by the central bank.

The bank borrows money from the central bank at, say, 0.25% interest (one-quarter of 1%) and charges the individual 4% for a home mortgage, or 18% interest on a credit card.

The individual is limited by his income in how much he can borrow. And should he fail to pay the interest and principal due on the mortgage, the bank will repossess his home.

Let's say an individual has saved $100,000 in cash. He keeps the money in the bank, which pays him less than 1% interest. Rather than earn this low rate, he decides to loan the cash to an individual who wants to buy a rental home. There's a tradeoff to earn this higher rate of interest: the saver has to accept the risk that the borrower might default on the loan, and that the home will not be worth the $100,000 the borrower owes.

The bank, on the other hand, can perform magic with the $100,000 they obtain from the central bank. The bank can issue 19 times this amount in new loans—in effect, creating $1,900,000 in new money out of thin air.

This is the magic of fractional reserve lending. *The bank is only required to hold a small percentage of outstanding loans as reserves against losses.* If the reserve requirement is 5%, the bank can issue $1,900,000 in new loans: the bank holds assets of $2,000,000, of which 5% ($100,000) is held in cash reserves.

Should 1% of the loans become impaired, i.e. the borrower defaults, the bank will have to subtract $19,000 from its reserves, as this loan will not be repaid. The defaulted loan is booked as a loss. Since this loss drops the reserve to $81,000, the bank must replace the lost $19,000 with additional cash. This is called *recapitalization.* The bank can either set aside deposits or profits to lift its reserves back to the minimum requirement.

A hedge fund, private-equity fund, corporation, etc. goes to the bank and borrows the $1,900,000 at a reduced rate of interest because the fund has assets to pledge as collateral for the loans. The fund then buys 19 homes with the money. Since the fund borrowed the money for less than the 4% the individual borrower is paying, the fund's expenses are lower and so the profits reaped from the rentals are higher than those earned by 19 individuals each owning one rental home. The 19 rental houses become assets that the fund can pledge to borrow more money to buy additional rentals.

The bank then bundles the mortgages and sells them to investors as mortgage-backed securities (MBS). Rather than wait 30 years to collect the profits from issuing the mortgages, the bank collects the profits as soon as it sells the MBS. The Bank can then issue more mortgages and repeat the process, reaping upfront profits on every loan it packages and sells as a security.

The bank's investment arm sells insurance against the possibility that the MBS will default, and reaps additional profit from the sale of these financial instruments.

This is a simplified version of how money is created and issued, but it helps us understand why centrally issued and distributed money concentrates wealth in the hands of those with access to the centrally issued credit and those who have the privilege of leveraging every $1 of cash into $19 newly created dollars that earn interest.

Let's list the differences between an individual, a bank and a hedge fund.

- The individual cannot borrow directly from the central bank. He must borrow from a private bank at a rate of interest that is an order of magnitude higher than what the bank pays the central bank.
- The individual must first save $1 in order to lend $1. The bank can use $1 to create $19 of new money/loans.
- The individual lender must wait to collect the profits from a loan over the entire period of the loan. In the case of a mortgage, this is typically 15 or 30 years.
- The bank can immediately sell the mortgage as a security and book the profit upfront.
- The individual can't issue exotic financial instruments to increase profits. The bank is free to do so, greatly increasing its profits.
- The individual must borrow at retail rates. The fund can borrow at much lower rates. This enables the fund to reap higher profits as a result of lower expenses.
- The bank and the fund can both pyramid wealth, using assets bought with borrowed money to buy income-producing assets, which then support additional loans to buy more assets.

How Money Is Distributed in the Centralized Bank System

Let's summarize the way money is distributed in the central bank system:

- The central bank creates money and makes it available to private banks at very low rates of interest.
- The private banks then leverage each $1 into $19 of new money, in the form of new credit/loans.
- The banks sell the newly created loans as securities, booking the profits upfront.

The major beneficiaries of the current distribution system are as follows:

- Financiers (extremely wealthy individuals, trusts, hedge funds) can borrow large sums of money at low rates of interest to buy assets such as stocks, bonds, rental properties, etc. Since they have almost unlimited access to credit, they can outbid the unprivileged who must save cash and borrow at high rates of interest.
- Those with access to central bank funds have an advantage over those who cannot borrow directly from central banks.
- Those who can create $19 out of $1 have an advantage over those who cannot create money out of thin air.
- Those who can book profits upfront and charge high interest rates have an advantage over those who cannot.
- Those who can borrow almost unlimited sums at attractive rates of interest can buy income producing assets have an advantage over those who cannot borrow huge sums at attractive rates.

The end result is as follows:

- Access to central bank money concentrates wealth in the hands of those with this access.
- Access to nearly unlimited credit concentrates wealth in the hands of those who can buy income-producing assets. Once the wealth has been concentrated in the hands of a few, these few will use this great wealth to buy political influence and favors via campaign contributions and lobbying.

No one disputes that the top .1% of households (top 1/10th of 1%) own 22% of all the wealth in the U.S., or that the top 1% own 35.5% of all wealth. (The top 10% own 75%, proving to these fortunate few that *the system is working great because it works for me*.)

This concentrated wealth inevitably subverts democracy.

If we ask who benefits from the centralized issuance and distribution of money, the answer is: the privileged few with access to this money. If we ask what centrally issued and distributed money optimizes, the answer is: *increasing inequality by concentrating private wealth which then subverts democracy.* Given the rules of the central banking system, *this is the only possible output.*

The following example illustrates this.

An Example of Pyramiding Wealth in the Centralized Bank System

Imagine if we each had a relatively modest $1 million line of credit at 0.25% interest from a central bank that we could use to issue loans of $19 million. Let's say we issued $19 million in home loans at an annual interest rate of 4%. The gross revenue (before expenses) of our leveraged $1 million would be $760,000 annually - let's assume we net $600,000 per year after annual expenses of $160,000. (Recall that the interest due on the $1 million line of credit is a paltry $2,500 annually).

Median income for workers in the U.S. is around $30,000 annually. Thus *a modest $1 million line of credit at 0.25% interest from the central bank would enable us to net 20 years of a typical worker's earnings every single year.* This is just a modest example of pyramiding wealth.

Next let's say we each get a $1 billion line of credit which we leverage into $19 billion in loans earning 4%. Now our net annual income is *$600 million*, the equivalent income of 20,000 workers! We did nothing to improve productivity, nor did we produce any goods or services. We simply used the power of central banking and fractional reserve lending to skim $600 million in financial rents from those actually producing goods and services.

Note that we are not uniquely evil or avaricious in maximizing our private gain from the central bank system; we are simply responding rationally to the system's incentives.

As with the example of the subprime mortgage collapse, the system concentrates wealth and subverts democracy not because participants are different from the rest of us but because they are acting rationally within the system. Would you turn down $600,000 a year? How about $600 million a year?

It makes no sense for banks and financiers not to maximize their gains in this system. Those who fail to maximize their gains will be fired.

I hope you understand by now that the current system of issuing money and credit *benefits the few at the expense of the many*. The vast privilege and the equally vast inequality it generates *is the only possible output of the system*. This inequality cannot be reformed away; it is intrinsic to centrally issued money and private banking.

The problem isn't fiat money; it's centrally issued money/credit that is distributed to the few at the expense of the many. If we want to limit the subversion of democracy, we must decentralize and democratize the issuance and distribution of money.

In the current system, money isn't created to reward increasing productivity. It is created to increase the wealth and power of the privileged.

If we want to connect the creation and distribution of money/credit with productivity, we must issue new money directly to those creating value and boosting productivity, bypassing the privileged few in central and private banks.

By concentrating wealth and power, centrally issued and distributed money doesn't just subvert democracy. It also *optimizes inequality, monopoly, cronyism, stagnation, low social mobility and systemic instability*.

Chapter Five: The Limits of the Market and the State

In our current hierarchical system, there are only three solutions offered for any problem:

- Create a market whose organizing principle is maximizing private profits;
- Issue more credit to the privileged few via a central bank; or
- Grant the state more power.

That these are not just incapable of solving the system's problems, but are in fact the source of the problems, simply doesn't compute. We assume *these must be the solution because there are no other options*. This is obviously a false assumption. There are alternatives, but there is no intellectual, financial and political space for alternatives in the current system.

The second section of the book will sketch out an alternative. But to do so, first we need to understand the limits of the conventional solutions: markets and the state.

The Market & the State Are Not Solutions to Automation & Degrowth

The open market and the state arose to serve specific needs.

A transparent market for goods, services, labor, money, credit and risk provides an opt-in forum of exchange that prices everything based on current supply and demand. This encourages trade and commerce.

The state (a national or imperial government) provides the political and social cohesion needed for collective action such as mobilizing the populace to defend against invasion.

But neither the market nor the state offer any solution to the consequences of automation, commoditization, globalization and Degrowth, i.e. the destruction of profits, payrolls and tax revenues.

The market can price the rising surplus of labor and capital, but merely pricing the surplus does not reverse the erosion of labor and capital's ability to create value in a world awash in labor and financial capital.

The state optimizes centralized hierarchies to manage collective action. The *creative destruction* of the current world system by automation, commoditization, globalization and Degrowth is not a problem that can be solved by collective action or centralized bureaucracies. The consequences are changing the nature of value creation, and this is a *different category of problem* than the type that states can solve.

In his book *Post-Capitalist Society*, Peter Drucker wrote: "Every organization has to build in organized abandonment of everything it does. Increasingly, organizations will have to plan abandonment rather than try to prolong the life of a successful policy, practice or product."

The state optimizes bureaucracies to prolong whatever privileges are currently in place, and it depends on the permanent expansion of consumption and debt to fund these bureaucracies. The state is incapable of addressing the *melting into thin air* of the world system it dominates because automation, commoditization and the exhaustion of growth and debt cannot be defeated by mobilizing an army or issuing more credit. As for banning automation—this simply speeds the system's slide to the graveyard of history.

Proponents claim that markets can solve virtually any problem simply by turning everything under the sun into a commodity that can be priced via current supply and demand. This is not a universal solution. Markets are optimized to price everything by exposing supply and demand, but this alone can't reverse the wholesale destruction of labor and financial capital's value.

Proponents of the state believe that if the state controls all markets, then it can solve any economic or social problem. But if the consequences of automation and Degrowth are systemically unsolvable by the state, markets or state-controlled markets, this faith that the state is the solution to every problem is not just wrong but fatally so.

If decentralized, distributed, self-organizing systems are the only possible solution, the state cannot be the solution. The most productive state doesn't attempt to solve problems that it cannot solve and limits its role to protecting the populace from exploitation and military attack.

The Market's Solution to Labor Over-Supply: Menial Servitude

The limits of the market are readily visible when labor is in permanent over-supply, i.e. the number of workers far exceeds the number of jobs.

Proponents of the market see lowering the price of labor as the solution to a structural decline of formal employment. This dynamic is already visible in online labor auctions (Task Rabbit, etc.) where the buyer selects the lowest available bid from the *commoditized* (i.e. the workers are interchangeable) informal work force.

All these forms of menial servitude for those who are not protected by the state or a private monopoly are theoretically offset by a parallel reduction in the cost of living that allows the poorly paid, insecure multitude to get by. But due to the state-monopoly structure that protects the privileges of *those who are more equal than others*, the cost of living does not decline even though wages outside these pockets of privilege are plummeting.

Is this the market working its magic, or simply the *exploitation of the asymmetry* between those whose incomes are protected and those who are at the mercy of the market? Is this exploitation of menial servitude by the privileged class truly the best use of this vast under-employed labor force? And if it isn't the best use—and clearly it is not—then what is the value of this asymmetric market other than *a pricing tool for the few to maximize exploitation of the many*?

The Limits of Maximizing Private Gain

What markets optimize is self-evident: *using all available means to maximize private gains*.

While private gain may incentivize positives such as innovation, it can also incentivize exploitive, destructive and unsustainable activities.

As an example: maximizing-private gain incentivizes reef-fishing with dynamite (especially if you can dynamite someone else's waters rather than your own) and hunting deep-water Bluefin tuna to near-extinction. (As the fish become scarce, their value on the market soars.)

Maximizing private gain incentivizes misrepresenting goods and services, designing in obsolescence (so buyers will soon have to replace the item), price-fixing cartels, and externalizing environmental damage by polluting the Commons, in effect offloading the costs of production onto the general public.

We can summarize the intrinsic limits to *maximizing private gain markets* in seven points:

1. The market has no intrinsic ability to discover the cost of long-term consequences, such as the future value lost when forests are cut down or the long-term risks of routinely using pesticides. This is an *ontological flaw*, meaning that it is inherent to the market's core mechanism of discovering price via current supply and demand.

2. The market has no mechanism to calculate the long-term opportunity cost to pursuing short-term profits. In other words, there is no way to know what other potentially higher-return investments were abandoned in the pursuit of short-term profits.

3. When a market economy is introduced into traditional societies, the incentives change from sustainability to extracting the highest possible profit from the environment before someone else does. If the market economy comes with a credit market (which it generally does, since credit is even more profitable than trade), traditional participants are incentivized to borrow money to buy luxuries that they could not otherwise afford.

   - Cheap credit profoundly skews our appraisal of opportunity costs, as the future costs of servicing the debt are masked by the modest monthly payments.
   - This inability to discover the price and value of anything other than the current price set by supply and demand cannot be fixed by regulation.

4. Markets are inherently vulnerable to elites seeking income that arises from control rather than from producing goods and services. Incomes arising from control—of land, borders, market stalls and credit—are known as *rentier incomes*, as they are a form of rent (or tax) paid for nothing but access.

5. Markets that set maximizing profit as the sole goal offer few incentives for adopting best practices or building intangible capital.

6. Markets are inherently prone to boom and bust cycles, as the exploitation of whatever is profitable unleashes a flood of income

which soon subsides as the source of value creation is depleted or undermined by competition. Participants are left with debt taken on in the boom and the external costs of a decimated environment.

7. Markets have no way to incentivize tasks that do not create an immediate profit—for example, monitoring the community's reefs to limit exploitation by others. It is presumed the state will step in to perform these tasks, but the state—dominated by self-serving private elites and state functionaries—has no incentive to pay for services to those with little political power, especially if the tasks might limit the profits of powerful interest groups.

There is nothing in the current structure of markets that incentivizes sustainable prosperity. The belief that the invisible hand of self-interest will inevitably foster a sustainable economy offering universal opportunity is yet another example of wishful thinking. Self-interest is indeed a powerful motivation, but it responds to whatever incentives and disincentives are present. If perverse incentives are present, pursuit of self-interest leads to exploitation and collapse.

The market economy can be constructively understood as a mechanistic tool in the toolbox of capital. The real engine of universal opportunity and prosperity is the *intangible capital* that generates a productive set of values, metrics, incentives and tools to build all forms of capital.

Earning a Profit versus Maximizing Private Gain

One implicit assumption in the current hierarchical system is that since earning a profit is necessary, maximizing private gain is the natural goal of all participants.

But there is a critical difference between *earning a profit* and *maximizing private gain*: a system that incentivizes earning a profit can still assign value to a variety of things other than profit. But systems whose only goal is maximizing private gain do so to the exclusion of everything else of value.

This is why Immanuel Wallerstein described the current world-system as *"a particular historical configuration of markets and state structures where private economic gain by almost any means is the paramount goal and measure of success."*

Earning a profit that can be reinvested or distributed to the owners of capital is necessary to sustain an enterprise. But this does not require the enterprise or its owners to devalue everything in the service of private gain. *Maximizing private gain by any means* inevitably leads to the sacrifice of whatever stands in the way of maximum private gain: the biosphere, the community, ethics and integrity.

Those seeking to justify their pillage of the environment, the community and the financial system invoke *earning a profit* as a smokescreen for *maximizing their private gain by any means available*. The two are not equivalent:

- Incentivizing earning a profit in a transparent marketplace can be part of a productive system that offers opportunity for all to build capital.
- Incentivizing maximizing private gain generates inequality by strip-mining everything and everyone to benefit the privileged few at the expense of the many.

The State Enforces Moral Hazard

The state has only one mode of being: *expansion*. It has no internal mechanisms for reducing its power, reach or control. From the state's point of view, everything outside its control poses a risk, and the only way to lower risk is to control everything that can be controlled.

By centralizing power, the state creates and enforces patronage and privilege. Privilege institutionalizes moral hazard, which is *the separation of risk from gain*. The key characteristic of moral hazard can be stated very simply: People who are exposed to risk and consequence make very different choices than those who are not exposed to risk and consequence.

The potential for loss (i.e. risk) is an essential input in decision-making and the allocation of resources, capital and labor. Decisions made when the risk of losing have been offloaded onto others are very different from decisions made by those with *skin in the game*, i.e. those exposed to risk. Decisions made by those with no skin in the game can be high-risk, because the risk has been offloaded onto others.

High-risk bets are generally bad bets. Systems that institutionalize privilege institutionalize moral hazard. These systems are intrinsically unproductive, because moral hazard breaks down the mechanisms that reward productivity and punish costly gambles.

When speculative bets can be placed by the privileged and the state absorbs the risk, the state enables moral hazard. In other words: the state = enforced privilege = institutionalized moral hazard.

The state also separates the consequences of failure, waste and inefficiency from those making state policies. Those working in state agencies do not suffer any consequences should the agencies fail to achieve their public purposes. Since state employees don't lose their jobs, benefits or pensions if the agency performs poorly, they have no real skin in the game.

The moral hazard that is institutionalized by the centralized state has numerous negative consequences. Authors Franz Kafka and George Orwell addressed these consequences in their writings.

- A lawyer by training and practice, Kafka understood that the more powerful and entrenched the state bureaucracy, the greater the collateral damage rained on the innocent, and the more extreme the perversions of justice.
- Orwell understood that the State's ontological imperative is expansion. Once the State has expanded beyond the control of the citizenry, it becomes the haven of those seeking to leverage its power to their own advantage.

Protected behind the thick walls of the state, the few are free to plunder the many without risk of consequence.

This is the primary lesson of the financial crisis and the emergence of *too big to fail, too big to jail* banks protected by the state and central bank.

This is how societies fail: centralized power protects the privileged few from consequence, at the expense of everyone else. We can now understand Wallerstein's characterization of the current system as *"a particular historical configuration of markets and state structures where private economic gain by almost any means is the paramount goal and measure of success."*

Any system riddled with moral hazard cannot boost productivity or distribute the gains from productivity widely, as gains are siphoned off or gambled away by the privileged few.

Centralized states are not characterized by corruption, favoritism, cronyism, too big to fail banks, fraud, embezzlement, sweetheart deals, insider trading, free-riding, unproductive investments, waste and endemic inefficiency by mere accident. These are the inescapable fruits of privilege and institutionalized moral hazard.

Where To From Here?

States, banks and corporations arose to dominance because their centralized hierarchies optimized the value creation processes of the 1st and 2nd Industrial Revolutions.

In the Knowledge Economy, value creation has shifted away from the previous sources of profit—labor, debt and finance capital. As commoditization and automation eat profits and payrolls, the growth of consumption, debt and tax revenues the system needs to maintain itself reverse into Degrowth.

The consequences of automation, commoditization, globalization and Degrowth cannot be reversed by expanding markets, debt or government power. These mechanisms, so successful in the past, are now destructive because the consequences are not at all like the old problem of shifting labor and capital from Industrial Revolution #1 to Industrial Revolution #2.

We now understand why the three pillars of the conventional narrative—central states, banks and *markets that maximize private gain*—cannot possibly be solutions; they are the structural sources of the system's stagnation, inequality and instability.

We also understand why the system cannot be reformed by adding regulations, i.e. changing the color of the jelly beans. Piling on cost and complexity simply speeds the processes of self-destruction.

Let's return to the core principles of the current world system listed in the Introduction:

- Money created by banks trickles down to create work and wealth for all
- Technology always creates more jobs than automation destroys
- Centralization is the solution to large-scale economic problems
- Expanding debt and consumption (i.e. growth) is the path to prosperity
- Maximizing private gain organizes the economy to the benefit of all

Each of these is false. We have found that the *only possible output of the current system* is a decline in opportunity and social mobility and rising inequality and instability.

The solution is to develop an alternative decentralized, distributed, global system that lacks the perverse incentives and protected privilege of centralized hierarchies.

Avoiding the self-destructive teleology (remember that word from the Introduction?) of centralized hierarchies that protect patronage, privilege and monopoly is an essential first step. But we also need goals that solve the core problems: poverty of opportunity, poverty of secure wages, poverty of capital, poverty of knowledge and poverty of purposeful, positive social roles.

Conventional anti-poverty initiatives have much to teach us about doesn't work: most fail miserably. But by focusing on data-driven results across numerous nations, Dean Karlan of Innovations for Poverty Action found that a six-step program initiated by BRAC (a large nonprofit organization) actually raises household income and food consumption— the most basic measures of financial well-being for those mired in extreme poverty.

The six building blocks of the program are:

1. A productive asset, i.e. a way to earn a living; for example, raising chickens, keeping bees, an oil press to process seeds into cooking oil, etc.

2. Technical training on how to make productive use of the asset, i.e. practical knowledge.
3. A small, regular stipend to pay household expenses while the new user learns how to make best use of the asset.
4. Access to health support to stay healthy enough to continue working.
5. A way to save money.
6. Regular visits from a mentor/coach to reinforce best practices, solve practical problems and build confidence.

We can summarize these into a single goal that is applicable not just to the poverty-stricken but to the entire social order:

A guaranteed opportunity for paid labor within a community structure that organizes meaningful work and offers opportunities to build capital in all its forms—financial, intellectual, experiential, human and social.

Based on what we've found in our analysis, we can also add a few more key requirements:

1. *The system's money is independent of central banks and states.*
2. *The community structure can be set up virtually anywhere at near-zero cost.*
3. *What's scarce—best practices, knowledge of what works, innovations and information—is available to every community group and member in the system.*
4. *The system operates an open global exchange of ideas, capital and commerce between groups and members.*

Fortunately, technological advances now enable the construction of just such a global system—a system that is entirely voluntary and independent of central banks and states.

Those Benefiting from the Current World System Face a Profound Choice

I have mentioned the built-in bias of those who benefit from the patronage and privileges of the current world system: *since the system works for me and my peers, it works for everyone.* Those who fail to benefit simply didn't work hard enough, etc.

There is more than a little irony in automation/commoditization eating its way up the labor food chain to the point where it is now gorging on previously protected managerial-professional jobs. The state-protected fiefdoms of higher education, healthcare and national security—long immune from competition/innovation—will either implode due to their high costs or be eaten by automation/commoditization.

Those clinging to the faith that the current world system is sustainable can only hold this faith by denying the self-destructive dynamics of the system. Simply put, the system requires growth to keep from collapsing like a supernova star: growth of payrolls, profits, debt, tax revenues and consumption.

Further expansion in an era of automation/commoditization, declining payrolls and profits, state fiefdoms, monopolies and debt saturation is simply not possible, regardless of what central banks and states set as policy. The era we are just now entering is one of Degrowth, not growth, and the current world system ceases to function in Degrowth.

If lack of credit and insufficient centralization were the problems, the global economy wouldn't be suffering from secular stagnation.

The current world system is self-destructive in another way. As we have seen, *the only possible output of this system is rising inequality and a decline in positive social roles*. Rising inequality—not just in society at large, but within each class—triggers instability which brings down governments, societies, economies and nations.

For poverty is not simply a financial statistic—it is a lack of the essentials of human life, i.e. positive social roles and hope for a better future. When the privileged skim most of the gains, this creates not just financial inequality but social injustice—an injustice that rankles not just the bottom layers of society but upper class members who suffer downward mobility as their more fortunate (or well-connected) peers take most of the shrinking pie.

Rising inequality goes hand in hand with declining social mobility. When the lower and middle classes realize the ladder to wealth has few rungs left, the awareness of social injustice becomes increasingly flammable.

This sense of being left behind or left out fuels social disintegration, and as society loses its cohesion, it also loses its ability to pursue (in historian Peter Turchin's phrase) "concerted, collective action"—the trait that binds societies and nations.

As Michael Spence and his co-authors noted in their essay *Labor, Capital and Ideas in the Power Law Economy*, the rewards in the Knowledge Economy will follow a power law distribution: the majority of gains will flow to the few who can provide what's scarce, i.e. new business models and ideas.

In other words, a world in which labor and capital create little value is a world of rising inequality, and the current world system has no solution other than taxing the few winners to fund the state-protected privileged. This is not a solution, it is a stopgap measure. The current world system has no solution to either automation/commoditization or the self-destructive teleology of centralized hierarchies.

 Financial, political and social instability arise together. History shows that financial inequality spills over into social and political instability.

Everyone who is benefiting from the current world system has a choice: they can cling to wishful thinking and be part of the problem, or they can accept that the only possible solution lies outside the current system and join those working on a real solution.

I lay out a complete systemic solution in Section 3 that integrates cheap, readily available technologies and social innovations that are in use today. So let's get started.

Section 2:

Designing a Radically Beneficial World System

Chapter Six: Requirements for a New World System

We've found that there are three systemic problems in the current world-system. One is that automation and commoditization are destroying paid work, profits and tax revenues. The second is that centralized hierarchies optimize privilege, a dynamic that destabilizes the entire system.

The third is the logic of maximizing private gain by any means available leads to the exploitation of labor, plundering of natural resources, predatory financial practices and the corruption of democracy.

The self-evident solution to these problems is to design a decentralized, non-state, non-hierarchical, global system that distributes secure paid work and capital while strictly limiting the creation and protection of privilege. For all the reasons explained in Section 1, this requires a decentralized, non-state currency.

In effect, *this new system integrates the creation and distribution of money with the creation and distribution of paid work and capital*.

This basic structure may be self-evident, but the devil is in the details: that is, what the system optimizes via its rules, what it measures and the incentives it generates.

The Essential Role of Crisis in Systemic Change

Profound systemic changes do not occur in stable eras and regions, for the simple reason that there is no pressure to make changes if all is well (or at least tolerable). Systemic change is only possible when everyone finally accepts that the current arrangement is collapsing under its own weight. Only systemic crisis opens the door to structural change, as those benefiting from the current system will resist anything that might threaten their privileges.

Since the alternate system I am proposing may not be allowed to arise in stable economies, the new system will likely arise in places where the majority are fed up and the Powers That Be are losing their grip.

This new system can only self-assemble if the state, central bank and cartels are unable to suppress it.

Ironically, the new system actually *strengthens* the legitimate state and marketplace. This new system's primary function is the alleviation of poverty via the expansion of income and capital. Rather than view this new system as a threat, an enlightened state and market would embrace the system's alleviation of poverty as a great boon to the sustainability of the state and market.

Establishing the Goals and Prioritizing the Outputs

To discover what the new system should optimize, let's prioritize the goals, which then define the desired outputs.

At the end of Section 1, we covered six building blocks of reducing poverty: productive assets, technical training, regular stipends, health services, savings and mentoring, which I summarized as: *A guaranteed opportunity for paid labor within a community structure that organizes meaningful work and offers opportunities to build capital in all its forms—financial, intellectual, experiential, human and social.*

I listed four requirements:

5. *The system's money is independent of central banks and states.*
6. *The community structure can be set up virtually anywhere at near-zero cost.*
7. *What's scarce—best practices, knowledge of what works, innovations and information—is available to every community group and member in the system.*
8. *The system operates an open global exchange of ideas, capital and commerce between groups and members.*

We can refine these further:

1. Paid work for all who want it by integrating labor, community needs and money creation/distribution.
2. A self-funding global system that creates its own crypto-currency, i.e. money that is not borrowed into existence by banks.
3. Maintain an *infrastructure of opportunity* for all members: anyone can start a new community group, join another group,

or operate an independent private enterprise while fulfilling their membership duties.

4. Operate a transparent market for knowledge, information, best practices, ideas, capital, goods and services that is solely for community groups and members.
5. Suppress the creation and protection of privilege.
6. Defend the system against theft, fraud and exploitation.

How do we design such a system so that the only possible output is capital formation and paid work for all who want it in a sustainable, decentralized global system that limits privilege and exploitation? Let's sketch the constituent parts of such a system.

The Role of Technology in Scaling a Self-Funding, Independent, Global System

Technology is the key enabler of this new world system. Not the technology of the future, but the technology of today.

The foundation of a self-funding system that integrates money and work is a network of peer-to-peer servers—in essence, computers that share data and resources with other computers. The world system resides not in a central server but in a global network of servers. This makes it resilient in the face of power failures, state attempts to shut down the system, and other disruptions.

Many commentators note that the Internet is not free, as the global network of servers, computers and mobile devices consumes enormous quantities of electricity. For this reason, some will conclude that the proposed global system will be unaffordable.

Five important trends call this conclusion into question.

1. Processors and digital memory are using considerably less power per unit than in the recent past. This reduction in power consumption is an industry-wide trend, and a focus of much research.
2. The current Internet of commercial server farms is optimized to produce nearly instant search results and transfer large video and audio files. But not all networks must optimize speed and transferring large files. A network optimized for low power

consumption would be slower and limited to text data and highly compressed photos. The electrical consumption of such a system would be an order of magnitude lower than the conventional commercial Internet.

3. Peer-to-peer networks are *distributed systems*, meaning the networks' software, data, processors and memory are distributed globally across thousands or millions of devices. This distributed network lends itself to equally distributed sources of electricity, i.e. small-scale appropriate-technology renewable energy sources.

4. Advances in processing power and memory coupled with sharp reductions in cost mean a $45 tablet can be a server if the software, data flow and stored data are simplified, for example, text-only.

5. For simple text-data transactions (micro-payments, text messages, etc.), data storage, and compact applications, low-cost smart phones already act as computers. These low-cost devices communicate with servers via increasingly ubiquitous mobile telephony.

In a network optimized for low-cost participation and low power consumption, community groups would need only a cheap tablet, a local source of electricity (if no grid electricity was available) and members with low-cost smart phones to join the global system. Even very poor households typically own a cheap mobile phone, and micropayments via mobile phones are already part of daily life in many developing nations.

It is estimated that the current commercial Internet (optimized for speed and bandwidth, not power consumption) consumes about 2% of global electricity. Let's say this underestimates consumption by 100%, meaning the global Internet consumes 4% of global electricity.

A network optimized for low power consumption would use an estimated 10% of this power, or 0.4% of global electricity production. This is considerably less than the electricity squandered on lighting empty buildings, not to mention far greater energy hogs such as so-called *zombie power strips and electronic devices on standby* which consume an estimated 5% of total electrical production while producing essentially no output at all.

If we consider power-hungry incandescent lighting and other obvious sources of needless consumption, it's clear that a global network optimized for low power consumption and low cost participation would consume an exceedingly thin slice of global electrical consumption. Many people seem to have forgotten that the Internet functioned perfectly adequately for text and highly compressed photos with very low bandwidth, slow processors and modest memory in the late 1990s.

It is equally clear that such a distributed network lends itself to distributed sources of renewable power, including photovoltaic panels, small water-driven generators, windmills, bicycle-powered generators, etc.

If we consider the enormous benefits generated by a global system that integrates money creation, paid work for all and a network for distributing capital, goods and services to fill local scarcities, the modest consumption of electricity required is not the stumbling block some might imagine.

We must also consider the incentives present when wages are paid via the network. Everyone with a payment waiting for them on the network will have a tremendous motivation to do whatever it takes to access their pay.

The Role of Innovation, Stability and Social Mobility

To generate a global abundance of paid work, the new system must distribute the engines of wealth creation: *knowledge* and *capital*. This requires a balance of *stability*, *innovation* and *social mobility*—the last of which, broadly speaking, is the pathway from no ownership of capital to meaningful ownership of capital. The balance is not easy, as these can be contradictory forces. Innovation destabilizes the established order, and the creative destruction that comes with innovation can upend old pathways of social mobility.

A productive balance of stability and instability turns on the distribution of innovation—in essence, *defining what the system allows to be destabilized*. While the new system encourages the improvement of best practices via innovation, the core functions of paid work and opportunities to acquire capital remain stable because the system's rules and processes are kept simple and changed rarely.

In other words, the rules of governance and commerce are kept highly stable, while the practices guiding the production of goods and services change constantly as better ideas and information become available.

The ideal arrangement is a stable set of rules with transparent governance, inputs and outputs, highly interconnected sources of innovation, a culture that welcomes experimentation and failure, and multiple pathways to distribute innovations. In other words, innovation must not be limited to a top layer of researchers; there must be multiple pathways for innovations to spread quickly through the entire system.

We can think of these pathways of distributing innovations as the pathway of social mobility, for distributing innovation distributes opportunity.

Nassim Taleb has described the irony of seeking stability by suppressing instability. An apparently stable system without pathways to spread destabilizing ideas and technologies is prone to collapse. All the attributes of long-term stability—adaptability, flexibility, resilience— result from the instability of innovation.

The Role of Transparent Markets

History has shown that the fastest, most efficient means of distributing innovations is a marketplace that rewards innovation.

- A transparent market for exchanging ideas and knowledge distributes useful innovations to those who can benefit most.
- A transparent market for exchanging goods and services creates pathways for those without capital to build capital.

Innovation cannot enter the real world of production without flexibility and specialization. Though we tend to think of specialization as the *comparative advantage* of national industries described by 19th century economist David Ricardo, specialization and flexibility are critical at the lowest level of economic production—individuals and households.

Specialization at this level is driven by the individual's desire for work that is rewarding to them personally and the scarcity of goods and services in the community, i.e. what work is most valuable.

Flexibility is a key element in bringing innovation to the real world. Specialization of the sort that is common in developed economies is not necessarily the most productive model. If I only have one skill, what happens when that work is no longer needed? If I learn three skills, I have specialized in a flexible manner. If I add a new skill to meet new scarcities, my productivity will increase because I'm providing what has the most value.

There are two parts to developing new markets. One is recognizing *nonconsumption*, a potential market that is undeveloped due to buyers' lack of cash or the high cost of goods and services. For example, when mobile phones were expensive, nations with predominantly low-income households were mired in nonconsumption: the demand for the phones was present but prices were too high. As prices plummeted to once-inconceivably low levels, even poor households were able to purchase mobile phones.

Alternatively, nonconsumption can be overcome by broadening the opportunities to earn income. The key concept here is that *distributing the means to build income-producing capital*, since the owner of capital has an income stream that is not dependent on the labor market.

The other part is developing innovative markets—markets that did not exist due to technological or social limitations. Recent examples include peer-to-peer networks and shared-economy enterprises that bring idle assets and labor into productive uses: car and bicycle sharing, etc.

Not everyone has the skills and talents that are rewarded by the profit-maximizing market. What is needed is a system that provides every participant a way to build capital and earn income within a parallel system of markets that are not dependent on profits.

The Community Economy as the Source of Social Capital

Given the dominance of profit-maximizing markets and the state, we naturally assume these *are* the economy. But there is a third sector, *the community economy*, which is comprised of everything that isn't directly controlled by profit-maximizing companies or the state.

What differentiates the community economy from the profit-maximizing market and the state?

1. The community economy allows for priorities and goals other than maximizing profit. Making a profit is necessary to sustain the enterprise, but it is not the sole goal of the enterprise.
2. The community economy is not funded by the state.
3. The community economy is locally owned and operated; it is not controlled by distant corporate hierarchies. The money circulating in the community stays in the community.
4. The community economy is not dominated by moral hazard; the community must live with the consequences of the actions of its residents, organizations and enterprises.

The community economy includes small-scale enterprises, local farmer's markets, community organizations, social enterprises and faith-based institutions. Its structure is decentralized and *self-organizing*; it is not a formal hierarchy, though leaders naturally emerge within civic and business groups.

Few Americans have worked on a plantation. I am likely one of the few who has lived and worked in a classic plantation town (Lanai City, circa 1970; I picked pineapples along with my high school classmates as a summer job). In my view, the current world system is akin to a *Plantation Economy*: highly centralized and hierarchical, devoted to maximizing profits for distant owners, a finance-fueled machine for extracting wealth from local economies.

We can differentiate the community economy by comparing it to a *Plantation Economy*. In a Plantation Economy, a once-diverse landscape of decentralized, locally owned small enterprises is displaced by corporations that are dependent on state support for their profits: direct subsidies, tax breaks, and a cartel or monopoly enforced by the state. The corporate Plantation's low wages leave many of its workers' families dependent on state aid to survive, and so it prospers on the backs of taxpayers who subsidize its low wages and the *externalization of costs* described earlier.

The current world system rewards those with access to cheap capital and the power of the state. The community economy has neither.

Contrast the finance-fueled, profit-maximizing, state-supported Plantation Economy with the thriving community economy of a busy Chinatown (not a tourist version, a real one).

Each store in Chinatown is tiny by corporate retail standards. In this small space (there may be only one aisle) one finds a full meat, poultry and fish counter with several butchers on hand, a wide selection of vegetables and fruit (usually placed on the sidewalk every morning), and aisles of canned goods, beverages, dried fruits, etc. Each small store has numerous employees to stock goods and serve customers. The owner or a family member is typically present at all times. If you stop to examine the boxes being carted in by hand, you will observe a wide range of local produce from family farms and local suppliers.

Next door, the bakery has several salespeople at the counter and several bakers in the back. The deli next door to the bakery has four clerks and four or five workers preparing food in the small kitchen.

This small neighborhood supports dozens of jobs, pays rent to several landlords (further distributing the revenues) and has multiple owners. In addition, dozens of small suppliers and farms receive a share of the revenues. Churches, day-care facilities, schools and playgrounds are embedded in the neighborhood.

This is the complex, interconnected ecology of small-scale capitalism, in which competition yields a rich variety of goods, services, prices and wages. This decentralized ecosystem is self-organizing and flexible; if an employer treats employees poorly, they can easily migrate to a competing store. If one storefront is vacated, someone takes the space for another enterprise. The state's role is limited to overseeing public safety and health, and collecting tax revenues. Since news travels fast in the community, anyone cheating customers soon pays a steep price as customers abandon that business. Choice and flexibility are the dominant dynamics in this ecosystem.

Contrast this to the plantation-economy's global supply chains that exclude small local enterprises and shift most of the profits of the supply chain to corporate owners. The Plantation Economy institutionalizes poverty, parasitic finance, externalized costs, moral hazard (since the corporate/state overseers do not live in the community being cannibalized) and centralized wealth and political power. *These are the only possible outputs of the Plantation Economy*.

Once the Plantation Economy has displaced the community economy, opportunities for work and starting small enterprises shrivel, and residents become dependent on state social welfare for their survival. By eliminating the need to be a productive member of the community, the welfare state destroys positive social roles and the inter-connected layers of the community economy between the state and the individual.

When the individual receives social welfare from the state, that individual has no pressing need to contribute to the community or participate in any way other than as a consumer of corporate goods and services. State social welfare guts the community economy by removing financial incentives to participate or contribute.

Why is the community economy so important? The community economy is first and foremost the engine of *social capital*, which is the source of opportunity and widely distributed wealth.

Social capital is the sum of all the connections and relationships that enable productive collaboration, commerce, exchange and cooperation. (We'll cover all eight kinds of capital shortly.)

Corporations offer a limited version of social capital—for example, meeting a manager in another department at a company picnic—but most of this capital vanishes once an individual leaves the company. This social capital is only superficially embedded in a place and community, as corporations routinely move operations in pursuit of their core purpose: expanding profits.

Corporations cannot replace communities for the simple reason each organization has different purposes and goals. The sole purpose and goal of a corporation is to expand capital and profits, for if it fails to do so, it falters and expires. The purpose of a community is to preserve and protect a specific locale by nurturing social solidarity: the sense of sharing a purpose with others, of belonging to a community that is capable of concerted, collective action on the behalf of its members and its locale.

Political scientist Robert Putnam has described this structure as a web of *horizontal social networks*. Unlike corporations and the state, community economies are horizontal networks, i.e. networks of peers connected by overlapping memberships and interests.

It is not accidental that the current system of hierarchical corporations, banks and the state increases inequality and erodes the community economy: *the only possible output of low social capital is rising inequality*.

Putnam identified a correlation between the inequalities enforced by oppressive elites (slavery being the most extreme example) fearful of the potential of egalitarian (horizontal) networks to organize resistance to the system and low social capital. Regions with low social capital are characterized by limited social mobility and rising economic inequality. In other words, the only way to lessen economic inequality is to nurture the horizontal peer-to-peer networks (i.e. the community economy) that create social capital.

This makes sense, as communities stripped of social capital offer limited access to the other forms of capital needed to launch capital-building enterprises and construct ladders of social mobility.

A vibrant community economy provides members with an *infrastructure of opportunity*, i.e. multiple pathways to building capital, gaining knowledge and connecting with others.

The key to broadly distributing capital and reversing inequality is to nurture the source of social capital: the community economy.

Self-Organizing Systems

The state and corporations are hierarchical by nature, with decisions made at the top of the power pyramid, and commands flow down the chain of command to every employee, soldier, appointee, etc. In contrast, non-hierarchical, decentralized systems are *self-organizing*; participants self-assemble in accordance with the system's rules.

An example of a self-organizing system is the World Wide Web. No central authority dictates the number of servers or mandates the number of web pages. The flow of traffic is routed according to simple protocols. Servers are added or subtracted based on the decisions of millions of participants. The protocols are managed by a not-for-profit, transparently operated organization, and are open-source, meaning that every time we enter a URL we don't have to pay someone for the right to use *http*. The basic web protocols are in the public domain, available for use by all.

Another example is the thriving Chinatown described earlier. No central authority dictates the rents, ownership of businesses, or the taxonomy of enterprises. If the number of restaurants exceeds the customer base, the number will decline as those restaurants that are losing money close. If a particular type of prepared food is scarce, someone will open a café to fill that need. The decision to test the market need is not made by central management, but by an entrepreneur.

Democracy is also a form of self-organizing system, because the participants choose an elected hierarchy to protect the Commons and oversee compliance so the few cannot gain at the expense of the many.

There are many examples of self-organizing systems, the most ubiquitous being Nature, which functions without a central command or hierarchical structure. Feedback loops and adaptive behaviors enable self-organization.

Self-organizing systems in the human realm must limit the pillaging of the few at the expense of the many. As a general rule, the costs of cheating the system must be higher and the benefits lower than the benefits reaped by complying with the rules. The two dynamics that destroy self-organizing systems in the human realm are *moral hazard*— the few offloading risk to the many—and *free-riding/fraud*, in all its forms: theft, collusion, embezzlement, shirking work while collecting wages, and so on.

Once the rules are flouted for private gain, the system loses legitimacy and it breaks down.

For these reasons, any system that creates paid work for all as *the only possible output of the system* must invest a significant percentage of its resources to compliance and oversight, to ensure that the costs of cheating/free-riding are much higher than the costs of compliance, and that gains from cheating/free-riding are lower than the gains earned by those who follow the rules.

Membership, Not Entitlement: Creating Positive Social Roles

The current world-system is based on *privileged elites* and entitlements that confer benefits but require no responsibilities. The guaranteed minimum income proposals discussed earlier are social welfare entitlements: residents are entitled to the proposed minimum income simply for living in the nation-state that issues the entitlements. Nothing is demanded of the recipients.

Though many see these two structures as entirely natural—hierarchies of the privileged few and *something for nothing* bread for the jobless— the basic human organization going back to the emergence of modern humans was a relatively small group of people bound by reciprocity and responsibility to the group and other members.

The core dynamic of this social organization is *membership* that is constantly earned by deeds and can be revoked if a member shirks his responsibilities or cheats other members.

Contingent membership is the essential glue of any sustainable system. Membership requires duty, participation, concerted effort toward common goals, placing the group's priorities above one's own private gain and sacrifice for the common good. Membership demands loyalty and labor; *something for nothin*g has no role in membership.

Financial dependence and the absence of a productive social order yields *social defeat*, which I define as the surrender of autonomy, fear of declining social status, and a permanent state of insecurity. The socially defeated, stripped of sources of dignity, self-worth, meaning, membership, pride and purpose, slide into a *behavioral sink*: as positive social roles vanish, self-reinforcing social pathologies escalate to the point of breakdown.

This black hole of self-inflicted suffering is characterized by self-destructive mental states and behaviors: chronic anxiety, resignation, domestic violence, self-medication with addictive substances, loss of empathy, the polarities of passivity and rage, and a spectrum of mental disorders from narcissism to attention deficit traits (ADT) and other socio-psychoses.

Social orders that excel in creating and distributing *social defeat* are populated with unhappy, depressed, anxious, and frustrated people, regardless of the material prosperity they possess.

Remarkably few commentators connect the sociopathologies of the current socio-economic order with the lack of positive roles in the social welfare state. But the sociopathologies are not accidental; *these sociopathologies are the only possible output* of a system of *something for nothing* dependence and a scarcity of positive social roles.

One aspect of social defeat is the emptiness we experience when material prosperity does not deliver the promised sense of fulfillment. A recent sociological study compared wealthy Hong Kong residents' sense of contentment with those of the immigrant maids who serve the moneyed Elites. The study found that the maids were much happier than their wealthy masters, who were often suicidal and depressed. The maids, on the other hand, *enjoyed membership in a trustworthy group—*other maids they met with on their one day off —and the purpose provided by their financial support of families back home.

Social defeat is more destructive than material want, as it cannot be solved with simple distribution of guaranteed minimum income; this conventional solution to joblessness exacerbates social defeat. The only way to combat social defeat and joblessness is to create a *positive social order* that offers a variety of positive social roles and mechanisms for restoring autonomy to all participants.

As my colleague Bart Dessart has observed, *a positive social order must demand cohesion, resolve, and sacrifice of its participants*. This requires *membership in a group whose purpose is larger than our own gain*, a purpose that demands individual sacrifice for the common good and a shared resolve to persevere in the face of challenges, losses and failures.

To design an ideal *unit of social order*, we must reach beyond the conventional models of state welfare and market-driven consumption and ask: what *coherent social order* generates what author Garry Wills called *public happiness*?

Public happiness is not just the aggregation of individual happiness. It is a reflection of the social order's success in enabling the common good, one expression of which is the potential for individual fulfillment within organizations that serve the common good.

To understand the centrality of the common good to human fulfillment, we must consider the social traits that benefited humans during our 160,000 years as hunter-gatherers. What traits were essential for everyone's survival? Cooperation in productive work, sacrifice in service of the group, celebrating windfalls with communal consumption, and leadership based on success and wisdom. Dessart describes the key trait as "interacting meaningfully with other people around them. Meaningful interaction means doing things for each other, relying on each other and at times taking risks for each other."

The ideal *unit of social order must fulfill all these requirements*. The system I propose distributes ownership and power to all members, and is governed by strict rules of membership and an elected chain of command. Private accumulation of capital is encouraged, but within a social order that prioritizes public happiness and the common good.

The organization of public happiness and the common good does not result from atomized consumers being given *something for nothing* but from a social order that offers positive social roles and opportunities to gain and contribute. Both are equally essential to human well-being.

Productive Work Is the Source of Meaning

States and corporations do not create meaning. Both are abstractions. The nation-state is a convenient abstraction for controlling mass populations, and corporations harvest the surplus of employees to benefit the corporations' owners.

The petit-bourgeois fantasy of every individual flowering as an artist, musician and creator once freed of work is also an abstraction, one born of the expansion of academic enclaves and private wealth-funded dilettantes fluttering from one salon to the next. The irony of this particular abstraction is especially rich: the more beholden we become to centralized hierarchies for our incomes and wealth, the more heroic the artistic expressions of rebellion against these same centralized hierarchies. But even these artistic rebellions are abstractions. Rather than generate meaning in a system stripped of meaning, these self-referential expressions of faux resistance and *newness for the sake of something new to consume* are parodies of rebellion and revolution. Artistic expression becomes an inside joke shared by self-referential elites—the very acme of inauthenticity.

Self-expression and consumerism are simply two aspects of the same empty abstraction. Once the emptiness of these abstractions is realized, all that's left is the individual's quest for solace in a world that strips away the very qualities needed for fulfillment, purpose, and meaning.

Humans draw meaning from producing, not consuming, and from belonging to a group that provides a larger goal than self-indulgence, which is the ultimate objective of consumerism. The profit-maximizing market and the state strip away these two essentials by turning producers into consumers and groups into atomized individuals fruitlessly chasing the chimeras of consumption and self-expression.

It is ironic that the system's class of well-paid technocrat professionals have internalized the fantasy of the market/state system so completely that they are blind to their own profound alienation in a system whose only possible output is exploitation, insecurity, anxiety, emptiness, unhappiness and the destruction of meaning.

Author Umair Haque neatly summarized this internalization of the system's pathologies in a 2011 blog post on the Harvard Business Review web site. Though he was addressing the pathologies at the heart of the corporation, the question he asks is equally applicable to state bureaucracies. Haque wrote:

"If you were to walk into any corporation, would you find faces brimming over with deep fulfillment and authentic delight – or stonily asking themselves, 'If it wasn't for the accursed paycheck, would I really imprison myself in this dungeon of the human soul?'"

The word *agency* describes the individual's freedom of movement and choice. In the abstractions of state, corporation and consumerist self-expression, agency is illusory: moving from one meaningless job to another is passed off as choice, and meaningless shuffling between forms of faux self-expression is passed off as freedom.

In the context of our previous discussion, work, self-expression and consumption have all been commoditized. Jobs are interchangeable, employees and employers are interchangeable, and various forms of self-expression and consumption are interchangeable.

The fantasy is that these commoditized roles generate meaning, just as the abstractions of state, corporation and self-expression generate meaning. But none of these create meaning; all are empty and alienating, socially, spiritually and psychologically.

The true sources of meaning are simple: authentic agency (freedom of movement and choice), membership in self-organizing groups, and productive work we can perform with pride. The current system is intrinsically incapable of producing these three requirements. Instead it strips away these three essentials.

The only possible outputs of the new system I am proposing are *authentic agency, membership in self-organizing groups and productive work*.

- Each individual has complete agency. Any individual is free not to join a group.
- Any individual can start their own group, recruit members and tackle productive work in their community.
- Any individual is free to maintain membership in multiple groups, operate a for-profit enterprise on the side or pursue artistic projects after completing their membership duties. Any individual is free to switch groups, or work for the state or a corporation.
- Membership requires following codes of conduct and fulfilling one's responsibilities to other members, the group and the larger community.
- Work performed in this structure is productive and meaningful, and as such is fulfilling and potentially even (dare we say it) fun.

Self-organizing groups that generate productive work are the foundation of positive social roles and meaning. A system of opt-in, self-organizing groups offers agency, membership and meaning as well as paid work.

Membership and meaningful work go hand in hand; they are two aspects of the same system. Membership and meaningful work are the foundations of human agency, identity, purpose, pride, fulfillment and meaning. This is why I say that *the future belongs to work that's meaningful.*

Capital as the Source of Secure Income

Capital is the only source of income that is not dependent on employers or the state. This is why the core dynamic in alleviating poverty is building capital in households and communities.

When we speak of capital, it is generally assumed we're referring to financial capital or the material capital of tools, factories, farmland, etc. But intangible capital—human, social, cultural and symbolic capital—is equally essential in creating value.

We can visualize the spectrum of capital by considering the process of building a house.

The building materials and tools we will use to construct the house are the *tangible capital.*

Imagine a group with no knowledge of construction being given the task of transforming the pile of lumber into a sturdy structure. They will be unable to do so, as they lack the *human capital* of knowledge and experience.

Human capital is both *intellectual capital* and *experiential capital.* Someone with knowledge of building codes has the intellectual capital, but if they've never pounded a nail or sawn a board then they lack the experiential capital needed to transform the lumber into a house.

If the group lacks the means to recruit people with the needed human capital, they also lack *social capital*—the skills needed to recruit, manage and collaborate with other people.

If the group has no knowledge of the local building codes and business practices, they also lack *cultural capital.*

If the group lacks the concept of integrating a variety of systems and building trades into the construction, they lack the *symbolic capital* needed to build the house.

The taxonomy of capital has been presented in a number of ways, and my version recognizes three basic types of capital: tangible capital (1 to 3 below); intangible capital (4 to 6 below) and two additional special types:

1.   Financial capital: cash, marketable investments, etc.
2.   Natural capital: the resources of the natural world including living capital (fish, trees, etc.) and resources such as minerals and fossil fuels.
3.   Fixed capital: machinery, tools, communications networks, etc.
4.   Human capital: the intellectual and experiential capital needed to make the other forms of capital productive.
5.   Social capital: the connections and relationships that enable productive collaboration, commerce and cooperation.
6.   Cultural capital: the political and social institutions that enable broad-based increases in productivity.
7.   Symbolic capital
8.   Infrastructure capital

Symbolic capital describes the conceptual tools that enable new ways of being productive to blossom. The concept of credit is an example of symbolic capital, for without the conceptual tools of capital, collateral, amortization and interest, this form of financial capital could not exist. The open-source movement is another example of symbolic capital, as is the crowd-sourcing model of solving problems or raising financial capital.

Infrastructure capital is the sum of all the other forms of capital working hand-in-hand. The sum of all forms of capital is greater than the parts. One way to illustrate infrastructure capital is to imagine a self-made billionaire being dropped into a desert nation with essentially no fixed capital, populated by nomadic people who have no interaction with the global market economy. Our billionaire's wealth, skills, knowledge and social capital would have no value there, because the infrastructure that supports these forms of capital is lacking.

In keeping with the principle that *only integrated solutions can possibly generate paid work for all*, infrastructure capital is critical, for only an integrated network of transport, communications, finance, education, judiciary and political rights—that is, the sum total of all the various forms of capital—can create a universally accessible *infrastructure of opportunity*.

If there is no mobility of labor and capital, no transparent markets for labor and capital, no creative destruction of inefficient systems, no decentralized access to credit, few means of cooperation, weak rule of law and property rights, or little room for innovation, if moral hazard has separated risk and consequence, and perverse incentives encourage cronyism, opportunities are going to innately be scarce. Virtually all efforts made in such an environment will be lost because it's a desert for broad-based opportunity.

This is one reason why cities offer so many more opportunities than rural areas: cities offer more access to credit, more means of cooperating, more mobility of labor and capital, more opportunities for innovation to take root, and so on: in sum, cities offer a much larger pool of *infrastructure capital*.

Back in Chapter Three we asked, what's scarce?

While we define poverty as a scarcity of tangible goods and services, this is generally a matter of *distribution* rather than absolute scarcity: poor people aren't able to buy the goods and services they need.

In terms of scarcity that creates value, we found that a specific subset of new ideas have become the scarcest form of capital in the digital age. (New ideas are never scarce, but ones that create value are scarce.)

Authors Erik Brynjolfsson, Andrew McAfee, and Michael Spence explained why in their 2014 article *Labor, Capital, and Ideas in the Power Law Economy*. What is increasingly scarce in the digital economy are ideas that enable new products and services that reduce the cost of inputs and boost productivity. The authors see innovative ideas as a *third form of capital*, with traditional capital and labor being the first and second types of capital.

Their analysis can be summarized in three points:

1. Digital technologies are radically reducing the need for human labor and the leverage of traditional capital (fixed assets and finance) globally.
2. Premiums flow to whatever inputs are scarce. Traditional labor and capital are no longer scarce; innovative, practical ideas are scarce. Ideas that enable new products, services, processes, etc. will harvest the majority of premiums/profits.
3. This distribution of premiums/profits follows a power law, i.e. the Pareto Distribution in which the vital few with the third type of capital (good ideas) reap most of the rewards.

As a result of globalization and overcapacity, most tangible inputs and labor inputs are no longer scarce, and so the high wages and profit margins that conventional labor and capital have earned in the past is trending down.

This mirrors the analysis of Immanuel Wallerstein on *Externalizing Costs*: for structural reasons, the yield on capital is declining and the cost of human labor is rising even as its scarcity value is falling.

Ordinary forms of capital lose value in this dynamic. Only the intangible capital of practical ideas and processes become more valuable.

Production, not consumption, is the wellspring of innovation and the source of income-generating capital. This is why the passive consumption of guaranteed income schemes is no substitute for building capital: capital generates opportunities for innovation, productivity and income. These are what lift people out of poverty.

The purpose of increasing productivity by building capital is not just to boost income and wealth but to *create a wealth of opportunities for security, pride/self-worth, purpose, membership and meaning.* This increase in capital and *full-spectrum well-being* is as essential as increasing financial income; the two cannot be separated, for the point of expanding capital is to distribute the sources of well-being—not just the physical necessities of life but the moral, psychological and spiritual necessities of security, self-worth, purpose, membership and meaning.

Though we in the developed world tend to think of innovation in a corporate context of new brands and services, the larger context of innovation is *appropriate technologies*: new ideas and processes that offer small-scale solutions. In a village without electricity, for example, capital that enables the sustainable generation of electricity from a renewable source (flowing water, wind or sun) has a great impact on well-being and productivity.

Practical ideas become part of humanity's *best practices*. While it is not possible to distribute fixed capital at near-zero cost, the intangible capital of *best practices* can be distributed digitally for near-zero cost. This digital capital provides powerful leverage to make best use of whatever tangible inputs are available.

As computer processing power and memory decline in price, even households with very limited income can afford a low-cost mobile phone that accesses the global network of *best practices*.

A system that distributes the intangible capital of best practices at near-zero cost generates a wealth of opportunities for security, self-worth, purpose, membership and meaning as *the only possible output of the system*.

What Are the Means of Production in the Knowledge Economy?

Broadly speaking, the term *means of production* describes the engines of wealth creation: tangible and intangible capital, and the structures of employer/employee, distribution and retailer/buyer.

As noted in Chapter One, author Peter Drucker identified the worker's knowledge as the *means of production* in the knowledge economy—an idea we explored in the section on the knowledge economy and cognitive capitalism. But as critics of this idea have noted, there is more to the means of production than a worker's knowledge. The worker with only knowledge to sell still relies on a corporation or government agency to provide everything else needed to create value: financial, tangible, and infrastructure capital.

Let's explore the components of the means of production.

1.   Knowledge and experience (human capital)
2.   Access to information (the network)
3.   Access to potential collaborators (social capital)
4.   Access to financial capital (to buy tangible materials and inputs)
5.   Infrastructure capital (everything needed to assemble various types of capital)

In the current system, everything other than human capital is provided by corporations or governments. And the poorer the household, the less capital that is available.

That there are few capital-rich alternatives to profit-maximizing corporations or the state does not mean alternatives are not possible. It simply means we must add new forms of *symbolic capital*. Once the blueprint of an alternative system has been drawn, it becomes a new model for assembling the means of production.

Let's sketch the essentials of an alternative system for assembling the means of production.

1. The system must be self-funding, i.e. it generates its own currency.
2. The system must distribute this currency to those producing goods and services, i.e. as payment for labor and organizing that labor.
3. The production of goods and services must be organized to meet the needs of local communities.
4. The system must support a global network for the free flow of information and best practices.
5. The system must support a global trade network to enable commerce in materials, goods and services.
6. The system must enable the free flow of financial capital, i.e. borrowing and lending between communities.

In this alternative system, money is not borrowed into existence by central and private banks or issued by a state; instead, money is created in exchange for the production of goods and services, i.e. the expansion of real wealth. Nor is this money created out of thin air to serve speculation; it is created to pay for useful work that has already been done. And this money is not created by a fractional reserve system based on debt; rather, money is only created in exchange for the production of goods and services.

In this new system, work is organized to meet the specific needs of specific communities, i.e. to address whatever is scarce in a specific community.

The system enables the free flow of best practices, knowledge and information to its members and their groups. It also enables trade of materials, goods and services between member groups and individuals, so groups and individuals can sell their surplus to the highest bidder and buy what is scarce in their community/region.

Those groups and individuals that save money can lend it to others in the network. This enables groups to accumulate financial capital in two ways: by saving a portion of their earnings, and by borrowing cash from others who have accumulated savings.

This new system is an integrated solution, a complete ecosystem that organizes productive work, enables the accumulation of all forms of capital and the free exchange of knowledge and goods and services. The goal of this system is to provide member groups anywhere on earth with the means to produce whatever goods and services are needed (i.e. whatever is scarce) in their locale and accumulate capital to buy the materials and tools needed to be productive.

This system is independent of states, central banks and profit-maximizing corporations. It exists independent of these entities but does not interfere with their activities. It is a new form of symbolic capital, a new way of organizing money, capital and labor that generates paid work for all who want it and enables community groups to accumulate capital without borrowing it from banks or begging for it from states.

One way to identify the means of production is to ask, what are global corporations able to do that households and community groups are not able to do? Global corporations are able to:

1. Assemble and organize the work of numerous individuals to meet specific goals.

2. Aggregate financial capital to buy the materials, tools and labor needed to complete major projects.
3. Assemble the expertise, knowledge bases and human capital needed to accomplish major projects.
4. Assemble the materials and tools needed to complete major projects via a global supply chain.
5. Influence political policy and institutions to further the goals of the corporation.

The alternative system I am proposing will be able to do everything a global corporation can do, and do so in a self-funded, self-organizing fashion. How does the new system do this? By enabling the global distribution of the means of production, so ownership of the engines of wealth creation is within reach of every member in every group.

We Optimize What We Measure

A specific type of symbolic capital is *what we choose to measure and how we measure it*. This is critical because *we optimize what we measure*. The process of selecting which data to measure has far-reaching consequences.

As a rule, whatever output gets measured is rewarded.

For example:

- If students' grades are based on attendance, attendance will be high.
- If doctors are told cholesterol levels are critical and the threshold of increased risk is 200, they will strive to lower their patients' cholesterol level below 200.
- If growth as measured by gross domestic product (GDP) is the measure of prosperity, then politicians will pursue the goal of GDP expansion.
- If rising consumption is the key component of GDP, we will be encouraged to go buy a new item when the economy weakens, whether we need the new item or not.
- If net profits are identified as the key driver of individuals' compensation, employees will endeavor to increase net profits by whatever means are available.

The problem with selecting what to measure is that the selection can generate counterproductive incentives. This is the result of humanity's highly refined skill in assessing risk and return, and recognizing the potential for a windfall.

When humans were hunter-gatherers—our natural state for 160,000 years, compared to roughly 5,000 years of agriculture—those on the lookout for a calorie-rich windfall ate better (and had more offspring that survived) than those who failed to reap windfalls. Calories were scarce, and the work to find food burned a lot of calories, so the ideal scenario for the hunter-gatherer would be a windfall that could be harvested with minimal effort. In the natural world, such windfalls might be finding a tree heavy with low-hanging ripe fruit, or a beehive loaded with honey.

In the abstract economy of the present, qualifying for a reward without investing too much effort is a windfall. As a result, whatever is measured sets up a built-in incentive to game the system (i.e. exploit short-cuts—or cheat) to qualify for the reward with the least effort possible.

- If students are graded on attendance, and attendance is measured by the students signing in at the start of class, students who sign in and then leave get the reward without the work of sitting in class.
- If grades are measured by a multiple-choice exam, students who steal the answers will get a high grade without investing the effort to learn anything.

Compare these relatively easy-to-game thresholds to difficult-to-game tests such as essay answers to semi-randomly selected exam questions. If the questions are chosen at the start of the exam and answers must be composed within the test period, it is impossible to prepare an answer (or pay someone else to answer) beforehand. Since the answer must be written in the students' own hands, having others answer the questions during the test period is also difficult, especially if the test period is brief.

Once the time and effort needed to game the system exceeds the investment required to learn the material, the incentives shift to learning the material with the least effort possible.

Notice that the system's cost of measuring data and enforcing compliance is correlated to the effectiveness of the enforcement. The more effort invested in obtaining meaningful data and eliminating cheating, the higher the value of the data.

In our example, the cheapest measures of student performance—attendance, multiple-choice tests, etc.—do the poorest job of measuring actual student learning. To actually measure student learning requires significant investment in the process, and a careful analysis of what metrics best reflect real student learning.

There is a growing dissatisfaction in the economics field with the current measures of economic activity (GDP, unemployment, and so on). This dissatisfaction reflects a growing awareness that these legacy metrics do a poor job of capturing what actually fosters sustainable, broad-based prosperity.

Does it make sense to optimize expanding consumption when resources are finite and the incentives to squander resources on unproductive consumption are so high?

If we measure academic achievement by the credential of a college degree, but the process of earning that degree does not measure or even require real student learning, then what are we measuring with college diplomas? What we're really measuring is not what students learned but their ability to navigate an academic bureaucracy for four years. Since we're not measuring useful learning, we have no way to hold colleges accountable for their failure to teach useful skills.

The success or failure of any system arises from our choices of what to measure and what thresholds we reward. Regardless of what we select to measure, participants will optimize their behaviors to reach those thresholds and the rewards they incentivize. So if we choose counterproductive metrics, we build perverse incentives into the system.

Rather than measuring growth, what if we measure the well-being of each participant and the opportunities offered by their community? What if we measure doing more with less, i.e. consuming less rather than more? What if our primary measure of economic well-being was the reduction of inputs (resources, labor, capital, etc.) that resulted in higher output (increased productivity and well-being)?

How can we identify metrics that measure well-being, efficiency, sustainability and opportunity? What thresholds can we set that will create incentives for adopting best practices and appropriate technologies?

To create a sustainable system that offers opportunity and paid work for all, we must first choose metrics that create incentives for best practices and disincentives for free-riding, cronyism, waste and fraud.

What Does the System Optimize?

We have found that centralized hierarchies optimize privilege— benefiting the few at the expense of the many. We've also found that maximizing private gain by any means incentivizes monopoly, exploitation, malinvestment and strip-mining of natural capital.

So what will an alternative system optimize? That depends on what's prioritized.

No system can optimize everything equally. There are always trade-offs.

- If you want to maximize profits, then you optimize hierarchical control and obedience.
- If you want decentralized, self-organizing groups, then you optimize innovation, messiness and *opportunities to learn and to fail*. Each of these is a slightly different aspect of the same dynamic: innovation is inherently messy and provides abundant opportunities to learn and to fail.

The trade-offs require compromises in whatever is not the top priority. For example, no system can optimize both innovation and efficiency, because innovation in intrinsically risky, messy and inefficient: many of the wells that are dug will be dry.

So what must be prioritized for the alternative system to be sustainable?

1. The system must be non-state, i.e. operate independently of the state.
2. The system must create and distribute its own money and capital.
3. The system must operate its own networks for distribution of information, goods, services and capital.
4. The system must make the cost of cheating higher than the cost of compliance. In other words, the rewards of compliance must be high and the penalties for cheating even higher.
5. The system must enforce simple, easily measurable rules on all participants.
6. The system must enable trustless transactions: the system itself must be trustworthy, so transactions do not require confirming the trustworthiness of each buyer/seller.
7. The system must limit the creation and protection of privilege.
8. The system must optimize innovation and transparency; in other words, it must optimize taking risks, messiness, and opportunities to learn and fail.
9. The system must optimize the free movement of labor, capital and information. Optimization of choice and movement optimizes messiness and opportunities to learn/fail.
10. The system must optimize the formation of self-organizing member groups and the scaling up of the network to handle thousands of member groups.
11. The system must generate incentives for members and groups that strengthen the entire system rather than undermine it.
12. The system must optimize decentralized leadership and innovation; rather than establish a hierarchy of leadership, the system must enable a dynamic mix of many leaders and innovators in a variety of settings.

In summary: the system must create and distribute its own capital, provide an immune system against the deadly infection of privilege, and encourage the messiness of innovation and adaptation. Such a system will enable the optimum human organization: small, opt-in, self-organizing groups that share resources and ideas while competing to best serve their members and address the pressing scarcities in their community.

What Is Money?

We all know what money is, but do we really understand how it works? It's not as easy as you might imagine, so this section will be challenging. But it's essential that we understand that *the manner in which money is created and issued concentrates wealth and generates poverty*. In other words, poverty is not just a lack of money; it's the result of the way money is created and issued.

If we want to provide paid work for all, we must design a system for creating and issuing money in which work for all is *the only possible output of the system*. The current system cannot do so, for reasons that are intrinsic to the way it creates and issues money.

If we want to provide work for all to alleviate poverty, we must first design a system of money that makes this possible.

Let's start our exploration of the causal links between money and poverty with a thought experiment. Let's say we could all create money out of thin air with a conventional printer or copier.

If I wanted to buy a house that was for sale, I could print $100,000 and offer the seller this handsome sum. But another bidder might print $1 million. I could counter with a $1 billion offer, and he might counter with $1 trillion.

We can easily see the consequence of unlimited money being available to everyone: money quickly loses its purchasing power—what we commonly call inflation. When money loses its purchasing power very quickly, it's called *hyper-inflation*.

Traditional societies maintained the value of money by choosing something scarce as money: in the far-from-the-sea Himalayas, seashells were used as money, as their relative scarcity made them valuable. In the South Pacific, sperm whale teeth were used as stores of value. Scarcity creates a *store of value*.

Money has two basic functions: it is a *store of value* (that is, it holds its purchasing power after you obtain it in trade for goods and services) and it is a *means of exchange*: there has to be enough of in circulation to grease the exchange of goods and services.

Though we are accustomed to one form of money playing both of these roles, there is no reason why each function can't be served by separate kinds of money—that is, one for exchange and one as a store of value.

This is precisely what we find in the historical record, where bills of exchange, letters of credit (in essence, *credit money*), paper chits from retailers and other ephemeral means of exchange greased trade, while gold and silver or other scarce materials served as stores of value.

The key feature of money used for exchange is that it *always has an end buyer*. The intrinsically worthless chit issued by a retailer can serve as money through hundreds of transactions because everyone trusts that the issuer—the retailer—will accept the chit as being worth an established amount of goods.

If this end buyer vanishes, so does the value of the money.

This is why many people have come to define money as *whatever the state accepts in payment of taxes*, as the state is the ultimate *end buyer*: whatever is accepted as payment of taxes is money. In historical examples, this has ranged from commodities such as bundles of grain to purely symbolic forms of money such as notched sticks.

Trust in an end buyer is the essential characteristic of money. When gold and silver were scarce in pre-Renaissance Europe, the great trading fairs relied on credit money—promissory notes, bills of exchange and letters of credit, each of which could be used as money because the end buyer—the counterparty named in the credit instrument—was known and trusted.

As anthropologist David Graeber established in his book *Debt: The First 5,000 Years*, money arose not from barter—the usual assumption—but from the rise of credit-based exchange and debt recorded on clay tablets, notched sticks or parchment. Money simplifies the payment of debt, and thus anything with an end buyer can serve as money.

This understanding of the historical way money was created—by issuing credit—helps us understand how money is created and issued today. Though we tend to think money is created when governments stamp gold coins or print paper money and place them in circulation, this is not the entire story. As economist Steve Keen (among others) has described, money is created when banks lend money, i.e. create credit, the same way pre-Renaissance merchants created money when they issued bills of exchange. When the bill of exchange is paid and the bank loan repaid, that money disappears from the system.

This is confusing unless we separate the two functions of money: *means of exchange* and *store of value*. Accustomed as we are to gold coins and paper currency acting as both, we forget that the vast majority of our money is credit-money: the actual physical money in circulation in the U.S. is a $1.4 trillion dollars, while the economy's gross domestic product is $17 trillion and the global GDP is $72 trillion. Total net worth of U.S. households exceeds $100 trillion.

In the Renaissance trading markets, money was created when a merchant sold ten tool boxes and accepted a bill of exchange from another merchant for the boxes. The most important feature of this transaction is the *money was created to match an expansion of goods and services*. In other words, although the money was created out of thin air in the sense that a piece of paper, once signed by both parties, was transformed into money that could be used in transactions by many other merchants throughout the fair, it was actually created as a result of the *ten tool boxes being produced and brought to market where their value could be established and traded*.

In other words, money expanded because production expanded.

Now compare this to the modern form of creating money. If a homebuilder constructs a new home, that produces value that did not exist before: a stack of lumber and other materials was transformed into practical shelter.

The home buyer usually needs to borrow the money to pay for the new home. The bank lends the home buyer the money by issuing a mortgage. The bank does not take cash from its deposits to fund the mortgage; if the bank has cash reserves of $10,000, it can issue a mortgage of $100,000 via fractional reserve lending. This $100,000 is newly created money.

Once again, we see that this creation of money aligns with the creation of goods and services—in this example, a new house.

If a government or central bank prints new money, and there is no corresponding increase in the production of goods and services, the expanding money supply is untethered from the real economy. Over time, increasing the supply of money in this fashion reduces the purchasing power of the money, as the amount of money that can buy goods and services outstrips the actual production of goods and services.

We call this loss of purchasing power *inflation*, but it is actually a devaluation of money. If money is only created to match the expansion of goods and services, inflation resulting from overproducing money cannot occur.

The old trade fairs' dependence on credit money illustrates another important feature of money that helps us distinguish between *means of exchange money* and *store of value money*. A handful of bills of exchange and promissory notes could enable dozens of transactions between buyers and sellers without any need for a single gold coin or other form of *store of value* money. At the end of the fair, all the credit slips were tallied and settled, and the difference would be paid in silver or gold.

The credit money might well have enabled $1 million in sales/exchanges, and the balance after all these many credit transactions were settled might be $1,000 in gold coins. So a very large of amount of trade can be transacted without a single *hard money* silver or gold coin trading hands, and the final settlement of all these transactions from an entire fair could be settled with a mere handful of *store of value money*, that is, money that is not based on trust in an end buyer.

This example from history shows us that credit money has a *very high utility value*, i.e. it is extremely useful, and hard money is not as essential as many seem to believe.

Another example from history reveals a key aspect of credit money and hard money. When the Spanish Empire conquered central and south America, it gained vast quantities of hard money—silver and gold. It seems obvious that this enormous windfall of new hard money greatly enriched the Empire, and indeed, the purchasing power of this hard money wealth was immense.

But the Empire found its aspirations exceeded this supply of hard money, and so it borrowed heavily from Dutch and other European bankers. Eventually the debts exceeded the Empire's ability to pay the interest due, and the hard money flowed north to the owners of credit money.

The point here is that *possessing store of value money is no guarantee of solvency.* Value flows to what is scarce and in demand. That could be land, labor or credit—whatever is in demand due to its *utility value.* Gold Rush miners in California placed a high value on fresh eggs, and money flowed to their scarcity and utility value. Value always flows to what is scarce and in demand, and it's important to differentiate between *demand for credit money* (means of exchange) and *store of value money.*

Though scarcity creates value, *store of value money* has an intrinsically symbolic component. The Rai stones on the island of Yap provide a striking example of this characteristic of *store of value money.* The large round stones (as much as 3.6 meters/12 feet in diameter) do not physically move from owner to owner as they change hands; rather, the ownership is maintained in oral-history records. A Rai stone in the bottom of the lagoon serves its purpose as a store of value just as well as one propped up in front of the owners' home. The utility value of a Rai stone is essentially zero—it serves no purpose other than as a marker of stored value, just as the utility value of a gold coin is low (what function does it serve? Perhaps it performs duty as a paperweight, but a valueless stone would serve this purpose just as well.)

This third attribute of money—its *symbolic value* above and beyond its utility value—is both mysterious and ambiguous. Money can be a marker of status, of esteem, of responsibility to the community and many other things. Though modern money is assumed to be entirely abstract, this is not an intrinsic feature of money; money can represent more than a store of purchasing power.

Money has a fourth attribute that we tend to take for granted: money is a commodity, and its value—in other forms of money, and in goods and services—is established by the supply and demand for that specific form of money.

If we say that *money has value*, we have to ask: *measured in what?* Though we focus on the ability of money to retain its value, the ultimate value of any money is its exchange value for assets, goods and services with high *utility value*: assets that generate income and goods and services that are useful.

Let's summarize what we have discovered about the two kinds of money.

1. The two functions of *means of exchange* and *store of value* do not have to be served by one form of money. Multiple kinds of money can serve both functions in a transparent market where the value of each currency is set by buyers and sellers.

2. Credit money functions as a means of exchange and store of value as long as there is trust in an end buyer of the money.

3. The value of traditional *store of value money* that has no real utility is a function of scarcity and symbolic value.

4. Scarcity only creates value if what is scarce is in demand.

What is demand? Markets of buyers and sellers—trading fairs, open exchanges—enable the expression of demand. In general, whatever has utility value and is scarce will be in demand, and money that can be used to buy what is scarce will also be in demand.

In some circumstances, gold is scarce and valued highly. In others, eggs are scarcer than gold.

Money is only valuable if it can be exchanged for goods and services. If there is no market of goods and services, gold is no longer money; its value is merely decorative. If a large market of goods and services exists but gold (or whale teeth, Rai stones, etc.) is scarce, then credit money serves as means of exchange because it has *utility value and is in demand.*

Value flows to what's scarce and in demand, and as a result those who control what's scarce control value creation and thus wealth.

So just who controls value creation? This question cuts to the core of the role money creation plays in poverty.

In the old trade fairs, two merchants who exchanged a promissory note created credit money that could be used by other merchants in the fair as a means of exchange for other trades. The note's value was based on the trust that the merchant would make good on his promise to pay the note at the end of the fair. In effect, the merchant promised to be the end buyer of the credit money.

Note that no central state or bank issued this credit money. It was decentralized and market-based; its value was based on knowledge of the merchants who created the credit money. *Their reputation accredited the paper as money*. This illustrates the critical role in accreditation and trust in creating credit money.

Now consider the way that modern money creation is limited to central and private banks. All the profits from creating credit money—the transaction fees and interest—flow to banks. Those with access to low-cost money issued by the central bank can lend this money at higher interest, or use it to buy income-producing assets. No one saving cash from an earned income can possibly compete with someone with access to low-cost credit money.

If we follow this logic, we must conclude that *the monopoly on creating and issuing money necessarily creates vast wealth inequality*, as those with access to the power to newly issued money can always outbid those without this power to buy the engines of wealth creation.

Control of money issuance is power, and so is access to low-cost credit. Those with access to low-cost credit have a monopoly as valuable as the one to create the credit money.

This reality has led many to see the solution as the eradication of credit money in favor of gold-backed money, so-called hard money that cannot be created out of thin air. But as I have shown, credit money has two essential characteristics not shared by gold-backed money:

1.   The ability to create credit money can be decentralized; it does not need to be centralized.
2.   *Means of exchange* money can be created in tandem with the expansion of goods and services. This gives it a much higher utility value than intrinsically scarce gold or silver *store of value money*.

The problem with credit money is not its nature (based on trust in an end buyer) but its current centralized issuance by a monopoly.

The key to the success of the credit money issued in the trading fair was *it was created only when the supply of goods and services expanded*. The supply of credit money was never infinite in the old trade fairs; rather, it was strictly limited by the quantity of goods and services being exchanged.

Since value flows to what's scarce and in demand, gold will flow to the wealthy who *control value creation* in the economy. In a credit money system, wealth will flow to those who create the credit money and those with access to low-cost credit money, as they can outbid cash buyers for income-producing assets, i.e. *the engines of value creation*.

We now understand why the current system of creating and distributing credit money generates poverty *as its only possible output*, as those closest to the money spigot can buy control of value creation. This cannot be reformed away by more regulations; it is intrinsic to the centralized creation and distribution of credit money.

For money creation to not generate vast wealth inequality, the ability to create money must be decentralized, and the new money must be distributed to *everyone producing goods and services*.

We can now see that for credit money to serve both functions of money (means of exchange and store of value) it must expand only with the expansion of goods and services.

This leads to the question: who are the natural end buyers in a credit money economy? In practical terms, *permanent demand* replaces the end buyer, and *relative scarcity* (i.e. the supply of money does not exceed the expansion of goods and services) drives permanent demand.

There are several pools of permanent demand:

1. Debtors who need money to pay off their debts.
2. Those with surplus goods or services they want to exchange for money.
3. Those seeking to borrow money to buy assets.
4. Those seeking the symbolic attributes of money: status, esteem, etc.

According to Graeber, the anthropological record suggests money arose to facilitate the payment of debt, so we can assume that debtors constitute one source of demand.

Though lenders may well prefer gold, Rai stones, etc., if the choice is to receive credit money or nothing, lenders will accept credit money.

Those with surplus labor, services and goods must exchange the surplus for money in order to realize the value of their surplus. Once again, those with surplus goods, services and time may prefer gold, whale teeth, etc., but if the choice is between credit money or nothing, they will accept credit money.

The magic of credit is that by borrowing from future income, a productive asset can be purchased today that will generate the income needed to pay the debt off in the coming years. For this reason alone, there will always be a demand for borrowed money.

Assets that increase productivity are typically manufactured, and as a result they are surplus goods to producers. If I fabricate vegetable-oil presses, and do so efficiently, I will have a surplus of presses I need to exchange for money. If a buyer does not have the cash but can borrow the money, his need to borrow and my need to exchange my surplus goods for money both create demand.

Human beings, being primates, construct elaborate pecking orders of status and power. As a result, some people will seek to acquire more money than they need for mere well-being. In many cases, status is earned by sharing the money with supporters or the community at large. Unlike the model of hoarding precious metals as unused wealth, establishing status and power requires not just acquiring money, but spending it in ways that benefit the group.

Scarcity and demand create value. If there is a large market for my surplus goods and services, and permanent demand for the money I receive for my surplus, scarcity is localized: a relative abundance of credit money will cause that money to flow to whatever goods, services and credit are scarce. Whatever goods and services are abundant will attract credit money from locales where these goods and services are scarce. The key requirements of this system are: open exchanges for ideas, knowledge, goods, services and decentralized money that is only issued when new goods and services are created.

A Thought Experiment on Issuing Money

Let's imagine a small mountain kingdom with only ten very scarce and thus highly valued seashells in circulation as money. These few shells are certainly valuable in terms of scarcity, but there aren't enough of them to act as a means of exchange.

One solution to this innate problem of scarcity—money has to be scarce enough to retain value but not so scarce that there isn't enough of it in circulation to grease trade—is for the kingdom to issue 100 slips of paper for each shell, each slip of paper representing 1/100th of the shell's value. Now there is enough money in circulation to facilitate trade and each slip retains a store of value equal to 1/100th of a shell. The slips are paper money, i.e. currency.

This system works well, but the rulers of the kingdom aspire to consume goods and services in excess of what their share of the shell-backed money can buy. The kingdom's leaders print another 100 slips of paper without acquiring a shell to back the new slips with intrinsic value. Nobody seems to notice, and so the leaders print another 100 slips. Note that the kingdom didn't produce more goods and services; its leaders simply produced more money.

Eventually this excess of paper slips reduces the value of each slip in circulation. What once cost 10 slips now costs 20 slips. This reduction in the *purchasing power of money* is called inflation, as the price of goods inflates if the money supply is increased while the production of goods and services remains unchanged.

Next let's assume the kingdom's leaders avoid the temptation to expand their consumption by printing money. As the kingdom expands its production of goods and services, the original 1,000 slips of paper are no longer enough to facilitate trade: lacking money, people revert to the clumsy alternative of bartering goods and services or issuing letters of credit. The purchasing power of the existing money might well increase due to the imbalance between the demand for money (high) and the supply (limited); what once cost 10 slips now costs only five slips.

Note that the value of each slip has now detached from the underlying value of the shell. It's not the scarcity of the shell that is creating the paper's value—it's *the scarcity of paper money itself* which is creating the paper money's value.

The kingdom can respond to this shortage by issuing more slips of paper. If the kingdom only issues a sum of money that is equal to the increase in goods and services produced, demand will remain high and the value of the money will remain stable as well.

But this detachment of the value of the paper money from the underlying value of the scarce shells worries some in the kingdom, and they propose that the kingdom borrow ten shells from other kingdoms and pay them interest for the loan of the shells. In effect, money is being loaned into existence: the kingdom borrows ten shells and issues 1,000 new slips of paper that are fully backed by the new shells. But the kingdom has to pay interest on the loan.

One advisor has an insight: rather than actually borrow the shells, why not just borrow the money into existence by selling the kingdom's *promise* of paying interest? Why bother with the shells when the only transaction that's needed is payment of interest on the newly created money?

And so the kingdom sells ten promises to pay interest—what we call a bond—and the buyers receive interest, just as if they'd loaned the kingdom a valuable shell. The new money isn't backed by shells at all; it's backed by the interest paid on the bonds. The kingdom sells off the original ten shells and issues ten more bonds. Now the kingdom's money is not backed by any intrinsic store of value; it is backed entirely by the kingdom's promise to pay interest on the bonds.

If the kingdom is prudent and only issues enough money to match an increase in the production of goods and services, the demand for money will remain in line with the supply, and the money will retain its value.

On the face of it, the kingdom's money has no intrinsic value at all; but if we follow the example closely, we see that the money is both a store of value and a means of exchange, and its value (when priced in shells, goods or services) fluctuates with supply and demand. The kingdom's slips of paper fulfill all the requirements of money.

When the kingdom loaned the money into existence, the money retained its value as long as the kingdom only issued new money to match the demand for money from the expansion of production and trade. In other words, the supply of money rose in tandem with the expansion of the real economy's production of goods and services.

The fact that the kingdom had to pay interest on newly issued money created a cost to issuing new money that eventually limited how much new money could be created. Creating too much money would not only reduce its purchasing power, but the treasury of the kingdom would be drained by the interest paid on new bonds.

This raises a very interesting point: when the kingdom created new money only to match the expanding production of real-world goods and services, it didn't matter that the new money was not backed by either shells or bonds; *demand for the money alone maintained purchasing power*. There was no need to back the newly issued money with scarce shells or interest-bearing bonds.

Economist Paul Samuelson observed that "money is a social contrivance." In other words, money exists to serve a social function— to facilitate exchange and the production of goods and services to the benefit of all participants in the economy. If the supply of money is connected to the demand generated by the production and trade of goods and services, it needs no backing by gold, shells or interest-bearing bonds.

The Social Value of Money

The idea that money has a quality that depends on its role and not just its ownership, on whether the money is stored away by its owner as wealth or used for social purposes, is alien to our current view that money is *ontologically amoral* and functions as a store of value, a means of exchange and as a signifier of power. The idea that the social quality of money is only present if the money is serving a social role doesn't even register in the current world-system.

But isn't it self-evident that money gathering dust in a potentate's vault has a quality and role that is quite different from money created by a bank to be lent at interest, and that both of these kinds of money are quite different from money created by the production of goods and services in the community?

What I am proposing is not just a new way of issuing money, but a new understanding that the *quality of money is defined by its social role*: how it is created and distributed, the role it plays in enabling trade in goods and services and the accumulation of capital. The social purpose of this new money is to serve the community and those laboring on behalf of the community. This new money is not amoral; it has an explicitly moral role and purpose. Just as labor is more than just paid work (as noted earlier, *"Labor is virtuous if it helps others"*), money with a social quality enables virtuous labor to build capital and serve the community.

Money created to serve an explicitly social role serves no purpose collecting dust in a potentate's vault. This money cannot be created by financiers for speculation, so it doesn't serve the interests of the wealthy and powerful.

As noted earlier, money is a social contrivance. The current world system is blind to the social value of money because it must be blind: recognizing that money could serve a social role rather than concentrate wealth in the hands of the few nearest the money spigot would completely disrupt the current world system.

From the Abstract to the Individual

It is easy to lose sight of the individual in the discussion of abstractions such as how money is created. These abstractions generate the day-today reality of poverty and powerlessness (social defeat). *That day-to-day experience is the output of the current world-system's institutionalized abstractions, i.e. the creation and distribution of money.* If we want to generate another more productive reality, we must redesign the systems that generate the day-to-day experience: to change the output, we must change the inputs and the abstract rules of the system.

We've explored the conceptual foundations of a new system. Now let's describe the engines of that system, and give it a name: CLIME.

Section 3:

The Engines of a New System

Chapter Seven: The Community Labor Integrated Money Economy (CLIME)

We've identified the structural causes of joblessness and poverty:

1. Wages paid to labor are in structural decline as a result of automation.
2. As profits and wages decline and financialization yields diminishing returns, the state cannot afford to replace private-sector employment with state-financed make-work or welfare.
3. Centralized issuance of money centralizes wealth, generating systemic inequality.
4. Centralized political power concentrates wealth and institutionalizes moral hazard. The few at the top of the power/wealth pyramid benefit at the expense of the many.

The current world system is a specific hierarchy of money creation/distribution, political power and incentives to maximize private gains. Community has no meaningful economic role in this world system. Not only is this hierarchy intrinsically incapable of creating jobs to alleviate poverty, it cannot sustain itself as the yields of centralization, financialization and resource exploitation decline. *Poverty and inequality are the only possible outputs of this system.* The current world system generates poverty not by chance or error but as a result of its structure, i.e. the system's mutually reinforcing hierarchy of centralized money, markets and government.

To create paid work for all, we must establish a new decentralized relationship between money, power, markets, community and work. I call this system the *Community Labor Integrated Money Economy* (CLIME). Though the technology to construct this system already exists, the necessary *symbolic and intellectual capital* does not yet exist. Section 3 describes this organizational structure.

Since the CLIME system does not yet exist, I should discuss it in the future tense—it will have, etc. I find this awkward, so I am going to describe CLIME in the present tense, with the understanding that it is a theoretical construct that could be a real-world system but is not yet a real-world system.

CLIME's Foundation: Scalable Web-Based Technologies

Many readers may assume that a global system such as CLIME is unreachably costly to build and operate. But this assumption is wrong. The present offers many models of low-cost scalable web-based systems with global reach:

1. Private sector non-profit management of global systems: ICANN (Internet Corporation for Assigned Names and Numbers), the Linux Foundation
2. Private sector marketplace for peer-to-peer buying and selling: Craigslist
3. Private sector peer-to-peer ranking: Yelp
4. Global non-state currency: Bitcoin

The technical foundation of CLIME is five integrated software engines (described below) that formalize the CLIME community groups, peer-to-peer accreditation, crypto-currency (*largent*), transaction clearing-house, and global marketplace for goods and services.

In effect, CLIME simply aggregates the four existing models listed above:

1. Not for profit management of a global software network.
2. Automated marketplace for peer-to-peer buying and selling.
3. Automated peer-to-peer ranking/accreditation.
4. Global crypto-currency.

It cannot be emphasized enough that *these systems already exist and are used by millions of people every day*. There is nothing in CLIME that does not already exist in some form today.

Given that the CLIME system is text-based, the amount of digital memory required by the five software engines is modest by current standards.

The number of people needed to operate these mostly automated systems is equally modest. Craigslist is managed by a relative handful of people. Twitter reached a global audience with fewer than 200 employees. These examples show that scalable, web-based, automated systems require very few people (compared to the user base) and relatively inexpensive computing power.

The CLIME system is distributed, meaning that local servers store community group data and the global software. The system does not require supercomputers or superfast response times. The primary system requirement is that the system is accessible to users via smartphone telephony or the web.

CLIME is a distributed, decentralized system, which means it is scalable. CLIME can expand from 100 groups to 100,000 groups with few centralized costs because each group adds its own server. Each new group contributes a small share of its income to the maintenance of the global system.

The point here is not to discount the complexity or the cost of developing the five integrated software engines; the point is to contextualize the cost in comparison to immensely costly infrastructures such as the global system for extracting, processing and delivering fossil fuels.

The five software engines and the computing power needed to run them would cost a small fraction of what is currently being spent on anti-poverty programs globally. As a rough estimate, a mere 1% of the money currently spent on alleviating poverty each year would be more than enough to fund the construction and launch of CLIME.

Since CLIME issues its own currency, it is self-funding after the launch of its five core software engines.

The Five Software Engines of CLIME

CLIME's global infrastructure is composed of five linked software engines:

1. Community organization
2. peer-to-peer accreditation/verification
3. Crypto-currency issuance, distribution and management
4. Global marketplace for goods and services produced by individuals and community groups
5. Transaction clearing-house system for the CLIME currency (*largent*)

Coding and management of the software is based on the open-source model of Linux, in which privately developed for-profit versions that use the open-source framework compete with free versions.

The accreditation and distribution of *largents* is performed by globally distributed servers and software. The community organization template is accessible anyone who wants to launch an accredited community organization.

These software engines formalize the five essential processes of CLIME:

1. Establish democratically managed community groups that follow procedures to prioritize local needs and address these needs according to best practices.
2. Accredit each group's compliance with the rules of governance; accredit each member's work so payments can be issued.
3. Issue the CLIME currency (*largent*) payments based on the compliance and accreditation of groups and members, and operate fraud detection systems.
4. Maintain a transparent global market for goods and services priced in largents, comprised of all accredited community groups and their members.
5. Enable digital payment/settlement of debt in largents, using mobile telephony and the Web.

The key feature of these five interlocking software engines is that they are automated. Decisions can be challenged and reviewed by members who have qualified to serve on audit/appeals panels, but the distribution of digital currency and fraud detection processes are automated. This reduces the operating cost of the system and reduces opportunities for human bias to distort the process.

The CLIME system is managed by an ICANN-type organization of volunteers with no financial stake in the system other than compensation for their work maintaining the system.

The one guiding principle is that there must always be a free version of each software engine, so that no for-profit company's version can establish a monopoly.

The Basic Structure of CLIME

The creation of jobs for all must be the *only possible output* of CLIME's structure. Since the core causes of poverty are a lack of secure paid work and a dearth of ways to build capital, CLIME must offer secure paid work and opportunities to build capital for all who choose to follow the system's simple membership rules.

We have established that any system has three parts: input, processes/rules, and the resulting output.

The input in CLIME is human labor working on behalf of the local community. Though it seems obvious that labor is the input, there are multiple dynamics in this simple input.

Physical labor may all the impoverished have to offer; their time and willingness to contribute is all they have in abundance. What is scarce is paid work, positive social roles, purpose, and ways to build capital. But labor is more than just paid work. As David Graeber has noted, *"Labor is virtuous if it helps others."* The purpose of CLIME is not just to provide paid work but to serve the needs of the local community, which is not an abstraction like *the state* or *the economy* but a collection of individuals, families and groups.

In the current world system, labor is largely servitude to the wealthy and powerful. The structure of CLIME gives every participant *agency*—a say in the community group he/she has chosen to join, and the liberty to start a competing group or join another group at any time. So the input is not simply time, but agency, liberty and a devotion to help others by contributing to the community in ways chosen by the community groups themselves.

This decentralization of decision-making is a fundamental feature of CLIME. In a fully decentralized structure, consequence and the risk of failure cannot be disconnected from those making the decisions. Moral hazard—the offloading of risk and consequence onto others—arises in centralized systems that have the power to transfer risk from the few at the top to the many below. The CLIME structure makes the institutionalization of moral hazard impossible. The community groups are free to fail or adapt to the valuable feedback of failure.

Decentralization of the process of creating and distributing money is another fundamental feature of CLIME. Money is digitally created and distributed directly to the individuals who performed work within accredited community groups. The group is not an employer; it does not control the money paid to members. The group has only two functions:

to democratically prioritize work to address what is scarce in the community, and to record and verify the work was done according to best practices.

Membership is contingent on meeting the basic requirements of trustworthiness and performing the agreed-upon work. The membership of individuals who attempt to free-ride, steal, etc. will automatically be revoked, along with the privileges of membership, i.e. paid work.

The process of verification is also decentralized. It is not a hierarchical process but a peer-to-peer process in which each individual earns a ranking of trustworthiness and integrity based on the accuracy of their reporting of their own work and others' work. Those caught free-riding, fraudulently claiming wages for work they didn't do, etc. will suffer a zero ranking of trustworthiness.

This structure is highly flexible and adaptable. A variety of community groups can reach a variety of decisions on what is scarce in their community. Individuals who disagree with their own group's priorities can leave and join another group. Individuals who feel existing groups are failing to address what's truly needed in the community can start their own group. There is no hard line in CLIME restricting individuals from pursuing their own enterprises, or working for more than one community group. CLIME encourages the building of capital by individuals, households and communities across the entire spectrum of capital. This flexibility of individual and community agency is a fundamental feature of CLIME.

The system requires an easily accessible, transparent market to buy and sell goods and services using the CLIME currency, the *largent* (pronounced *lahr-jah-nt* by those who recognize its French root, or *largent* in English). This system must be open to those outside the CLIME system as well, so those within the system can sell any surplus in the outside marketplace and buy goods and services produced outside the system. Those outside the system can choose to sell their surplus goods and services to those within the CLIME system for *largents*, or establish a currency exchange that trades *largents* for other currencies.

The sole requirement is that individuals and groups within the CLIME system must accept *largents* for whatever they sell in the CLIME system. They are free to demand whatever they want from outside buyers and sellers, but within the system, they must accept *largents* for payments of debt and purchases. The price they ask or pay in *largents* is up to each individual or group.

In other words, it is a decentralized free market.

As a result of this highly decentralized structure, *the CLIME system is extremely messy, chaotic and dynamic*. This fundamental dynamism is not formally specified—it arises out of the freedom and decentralization of the system's structure. These characteristics generate the system's resiliency, adaptability, flexibility and productivity.

Since the system generates paid work for everyone who chooses to participate and enables the building of capital by individuals, households and communities, the *only possible output* of the CLIME structure is greater income, more capital, more financial security and greater well-being.

The Key Innovations of CLIME

The CLIME system embodies several key innovations.

1. The crypto-currency, the *largent*, is a *labor-backed currency*. It cannot be issued in near-infinite quantities like central bank currencies, nor can it be loaned into existence like credit in fractional-reserve banking. It is intrinsically limited to the amount of accredited labor performed by members in accredited community groups.

    The largent cannot be funneled to cronies or elites; it is distributed directly to each member whose work qualifies for payment, and to those performing work for the CLIME system itself.

2. The *peer-to-peer accreditation system* establishes the trustworthiness of all participants based on the verified results of their work and the accuracy of their accreditation of peers. Digital evidence of completed work—for example, low-resolution photos submitted by third parties—are correlated with verification submitted by peers. Those who fabricate claims or falsely accredit

others lose their own trustworthiness ranking and membership privileges.

This system enables participants *to accredit their own skills and trustworthiness*, a type of social capital that they can take with them to other groups. I call this mechanism *accredit yourself*, as the power to earn a high rating of integrity is available to each member.

The system is self-funding: the labor required to operate the CLIME system is paid in *largents*. The development and management of the software engines does not rely on volunteers, as in many open-source software projects, or on venture capital; contributors are paid in largents issued by the system itself. For-profit versions of the software are encouraged, with the only stipulation being the owners of third-party versions will also be paid in *largents*. The system does not require external funding or unpaid labor; all it requires is a market for goods and services priced in *largents*.

3. The global market for goods and services priced in *largents* is enabled by *the CLIME marketplace* (similar to Craigslist listings of goods and services for sale) *but is not limited to the CLIME marketplace*; any CLIME member is free to trade their *largents* or products in an outside market.

The Principles of CLIME

CLIME's core processes and rules embody the following principles:

1. The system must incentivize the adoption of best practices (promoting productivity and sustainability) and building capital in households and the community.
2. The system must disincentivize free-riding, cheating and fraud by insuring the cost of cheating is higher than the cost of compliance and the benefit of cheating is lower than the payoffs of membership.
3. The system must eradicate moral hazard by eliminating opportunities for politicization, bias and cronyism via automated software that is transparently overseen by a decentralized, open-source network.

4. The system must issue newly created money directly to individuals who perform labor within an accredited community group, as well as to those working to maintain/develop the CLIME systems. In other words, *the system is self-funding,* and needs no outside investment beyond its initial launch.
5. The system must establish a structure of individual membership in democratically governed community groups that continually verify their compliance with the system's rules of governance. Individuals and groups that fail to follow the basic code of conduct lose their membership and accreditation and the privilege to participate in CLIME.
6. The system must set up a low-cost procedure for starting a new community group so that virtually any individual can start a new group that competes with existing groups. Participants are free to leave one community group in favor of another, join more than one group, or start a competing group.
7. The system must define the procedure groups follow to democratically discover what is scarce in the community, and organize the membership's workforce to address these needs.
8. The system must establish a low-cost financial clearinghouse so members can settle payments and transfers (purchases, debts, loans, etc.) securely within the CLIME system.
9. The system must operate a global marketplace for goods and services produced by individuals, households and groups within CLIME that is also open to the outside marketplace.
10. The system must institutionalize a peer-to-peer accreditation mechanism that enables each individual and group to establish a transparent public ranking of integrity and trustworthiness.
11. The system must set up an audit/appeal process to settle claims that the automated system inaccurately voided accreditation or payments.
12. The system's software must be structured so the primary source code is in the public domain, but that for-profit developers are welcome to produce competing versions.

One foundational principle of the CLIME/largent system is that it is not beholden to any state or for-profit corporation. It needs no one's approval to operate globally.

The Many Opportunities for For-Profit Enterprises in CLIME

CLIME welcomes for-profit competitors to provide services for CLIME groups and members. There is nothing in CLIME that limits for-profit enterprises of any size from offering services to CLIME members. The only system requirements are:

1. All service providers must accept payment in full in largents
2. The managing board of CLIME must retain ownership and licensing rights to a free version of the five software engines.

Ideally, a number of for-profit enterprises will offer competing payment clearinghouse services, foreign exchange services, etc. to CLIME members. Other enterprises could offer a wide range of other services within CLIME, for everything from software wizards to guide neophytes through the process of setting up a CLIME group to system-wide anti-fraud services.

A core tenet of CLIME is that competition is essential to boost productivity and offer members the widest possible range of opportunities. CLIME groups and members are free to offer for-profit services to both CLIME and outside markets. There are three system requirements for groups and members:

1. All goods and services must be offered to CLIME groups and members, i.e. no goods or services can be offered exclusively to non-CLIME markets, and all CLIME sellers must accept payment in full in largents.
2. Any for-profit production must be secondary to projects that address the most pressing needs of the community.
3. All CLIME groups and members must accept largents as the preferred currency, even from outside buyers and vendors.

The system lends itself to turning a profit on any surplus production. For example, a CLIME group that democratically selects improving the quantity and quality of locally grown foods in the community as their first priority is free to sell any surplus to other CLIME groups or to outside vendors for largents.

This systemic preference for largents supports demand for largents, which in turn supports the currency's purchasing power. If outside buyers have no largents for payment, surplus can be sold in exchange for any other cash currency.

Individual members are allowed to operate for-profit enterprises while being members of a CLIME group. The only requirement is that members fulfill the work responsibilities they accepted upon membership. The system encourages households to operate privately owned enterprises after they've completed their work duties in the group.

Competition and transparency are the lifeblood of the CLIME system: competition between service providers and between groups.

The Organizational Structure of CLIME

Those familiar with the World Wide Web will quickly grasp the basic organizational structure of CLIME, which is essentially a globally distributed network of servers that run the five software engines that track CLIME groups and members, issue largents and store data. In effect, each accredited group becomes a node in the CLIME network. As the network of groups and members grows, servers are added to handle the increasing data.

Each unit of the largent currency is identifiable by a code—a string of alphanumeric symbols. This enables every unit of currency to be tracked and verified. This also enables units of currency that have been fraudulently obtained or obtained by force to be deleted from the system.

Unlike bitcoin, which is digitally mined, the largent is created by CLIME servers when payment for labor is issued directly to a member of an accredited group. The unique digital identity of each unit enables each member to store his/her largents in a CLIME account that can be accessed by any mobile phone or networked device, and used to make and receive payments from other CLIME members and groups.

In essence, CLIME is enabled by inexpensive memory and processing power and its reliance on simple alphanumeric data.

We can visualize the CLIME system as having four layers:

1. The technological layer of servers and automated software that enable the largent, the accreditation of groups, payments to individuals, system integrity/security and fraud detection.
2. Groups that meet the standards of transparency and governance.
3. Individual members, who are free to leave or join groups or launch their own group.
4. The administrators of the technological layer and members who volunteer to serve on audit/appeals boards that resolve claims and disputes regarding voided payments, canceled memberships, etc.

The Incentive Structure of CLIME

Like all organisms, humans have been selected over millennia to seek windfalls that yield a surplus of calories/power/safety at little to no cost. In the modern world, this can be seen in the desire for *something for nothing* or *free money*.

If CLIME did not require productive work, the currency would not be tied to the production of goods and services, and all the work that is not performed for profit or by the state would go undone. That this work is not being done is a key dynamic of poverty.

If CLIME requires productive work be accomplished but does not enforce this fundamental principle, the entire system would soon lose its legitimacy, as those who worked would be derided as suckers by those who received the benefits of membership without contributing anything, i.e. free-riding. To ensure the system's integrity and legitimacy, the basic principle of pay for work already done must be strictly enforced with zero-tolerance for cheating, fraud or misrepresentation of work performed. And to ensure system integrity, CLIME must make it *easy to comply and difficult to cheat.* This requires the system allocate significant resources to fraud detection and verification.

Systemically, *the barriers to entry are low, but the barriers to fraud are high.* Those with no track record of trustworthiness are given the opportunity to prove themselves, and the peer-to-peer system assigns a rating based on the accuracy of their reports, i.e. how well their reports align with those who have a high rating.

Those who are discovered to be exaggerating the work performed by themselves or their cronies will lose their pay and membership, and their ranking of trustworthiness will drop to zero. This will alert other members and make it difficult for the cheater to gain membership in other groups. Loss of income, membership and trustworthiness are severe disincentives to cheating, fraud, etc., as each individual's rating of trustworthiness is public. And since those who place their own trustworthiness at risk by accrediting a free-rider also have their ranking reduced to zero and their pay and membership voided when the fraud is discovered, cheaters will find it difficult to persuade others to support their false claims.

The incentives to maintain one's ranking of trustworthiness/integrity and the privileges of membership are significant: secure income, positive feedback of work that improve the lives of those in the community, opportunities to learn new skills (human capital), saving money (financial capital)—the list is long, and complying with the rules of working productively with others and filing accurate reports is not difficult. In other words, the standards of conduct in CLIME are similar to those of a for-profit global corporation: free-riding, cheating, fraud, etc. are recognized as toxic to the work environment and the legitimacy of the company.

Dysfunctional societies have long reinforced free-riding, cheating, gaming the system, bribery, fraud, cronyism, etc., and those accustomed to benefiting from these anti-social behaviors will likely experience a culture shock when the behaviors they were able to get away with outside CLIME are quickly punished within CLIME.

We can anticipate a difficult period of adjustment when CLIME groups are established in dysfunctional societies, and people find the automated fraud detection systems cannot be bribed or threatened.

Those who succeed in fraudulently obtaining *largents* will quickly find the theft is not like stealing paper currency or other kinds of money; the ill-gotten *largents* are immediately frozen by the fraud detection software, along with any other *largents* held by the thief.

Given the difficulty is finding another group that will accept known cheaters as members, the losses incurred by anyone free-riding or stealing are significant, as the transparency of the peer-to-peer accreditation system makes it difficult to enter another group. Adopting a new identity means starting with a zero trustworthiness ranking, and many groups will naturally refuse applicants who have a suspiciously blank peer-to-peer ranking.

Humans are highly attuned to injustice, and as a result the system anticipates the response of those who have worked hard when they observe theft, fraud or free-riding: witnesses can notify the system with an anonymous SMS text or email message. The system's automated fraud detection program scans the records and peer-to-peer accreditation of the individual and group in question. If there is any ambiguity or suspicion, the system freezes the accounts of the individual and the group and then launches an audit by randomly selecting auditors from a pool of volunteers (always from outside the group in question) to ensure an unbiased investigation.

The wide base of the peer-to-peer system makes it difficult for a vindictive enemy to sabotage someone's ranking. The fraud detection software is alert to malcontents, and those filing repeated verifiably false accusations will lose their membership and ranking just like those who make false work claims.

Those who volunteer to serve in the audit pool never know what case they will be assigned or which other auditors they will work with. This makes it extremely difficult to rig the audit to overlook fraud/theft.

Any member who reports theft/fraud receives a reward once the theft is verified, as does his/her group. This rewarding of those who protect the integrity of the system expresses one of the key principles of CLIME: *those who cheat the system cheat every member*.

Those Who Cheat the System Cheat Every Member

Every organization has slogans that embody core principles. One slogan of CLIME is *those who cheat the system cheat each member*. In the existing centralized hierarchy, those who free-ride, cheat or commit fraud generally justify their theft in two ways: *everybody else is doing it, too*, and *I'm not hurting anyone* - in other words, cheating the system doesn't hurt anyone. This amorality is implicit in a system based on maximizing private gain by any means available.

The CLIME system has an explicit moral context: the system only works if every member is held to the same standard. In CLIME, nobody is allowed to get away with free-riding, theft or fraud, and so it isn't true that *everybody else is doing it, too*.

Every member and group is repeatedly told that *those who cheat the system cheat every member* because this is fact: every theft or fraud that goes undetected reduces trust in the system and dilutes the value of largents. Each member must understand that there is no victimless theft in CLIME; the system only works if there is zero-tolerance for lying, misrepresentation, free-riding, theft and fraud. This is a moral absolute that is reinforced by rewarding those who report theft/fraud and the immediate revocation of membership of everyone who cheats or defrauds the system. Stated another way: *getting away with theft and fraud is a form of privilege* that undermines the system.

The Garden Analogy

From a moral perspective, we can say that the incentive structure rewards good behavior and punishes bad behavior, but this does not capture the core purpose of the incentive structure. We can best understand the incentive structure of CLIME with a garden analogy. (Those who are not gardeners will have to forgive my predilection for messy but productive gardening.)

In effect, the CLIME system is a community garden for those who are not prospering in the current world system. Individual efforts in CLIME benefit both the individual and the community, as the garden expands and becomes more bountiful as a result of individual efforts. The community garden attracts pollinators (insects) that benefit each individual gardener, as well as other gardeners. It is a classic virtuous cycle.

Entrenched poverty is like hard-pan soil—nothing grows on the rock-hard ground which more closely resembles concrete than fertile soil. As noted earlier, social orders with no *infrastructure of opportunity* are deserts for initiative, innovation and the creation of income and capital by the non-privileged.

The CLIME system is the equivalent of a thousand spoons being applied to the rock-hard ground, slowly scraping the lifeless soil to create holes in the hard-pan large enough for compost and a seed. With careful watering and care, a thousand productive plants take hold in the once-lifeless soil. A hand trowel that bounced fruitlessly off the rock-hard ground now sinks into the soft, fertile soil surrounding each plant.

There are those who cannot imagine the hard-pan becoming fertile. Others resent efforts to make the hard-pan fertile, for a variety of self-defeating reasons. Unenlightened states will try to stop the project out of fear that the newly empowered gardeners will threaten the privileges of the few. Still others will claim it is impossible to turn the hard-pan into a garden without a million-dollar tractor, well-paid experts, special seeds and millions of dollars in high-interest loans.

All are wrong. All it takes is a thousand spoons chipping away at the dysfunctional hard-pan of jobless poverty every day, supported by a system that provides the organization, compost, seeds and water.

The Network Effect

Clearly, a single CLIME group starting in a single community will not have a *trading circle* of other largent-funded groups to trade with, so the largents earned by the single group's members will have no trading value. (I am indebted to Jeff Williams for the term *trading circle* to describe a marketplace of members.) The CLIME system only works if there is a trading circle of many groups. It thus becomes critical to add groups and members as quickly as possible to expand the goods and services that are being created and offered for sale.

The *network effect* is central to the CLIME system: every group and member that is added increases the value of the entire system. The success of CLIME in one area will provide a path for others to follow. The Network Effect is perhaps the single most important factor in the initial success or failure of CLIME.

As noted in *The Essential Role of Crisis in Systemic Change*, the impetus to form CLIME groups will likely arise as a result of crisis that cripples a nation or region. As the current system fails, people will increasingly be willing to risk investing their time and energy in a CLIME group.

Ideally, a faith-based or non-governmental organization (NGO) organizes multiple CLIME groups in one campaign. For-profit companies could pursue the same goal as a pathway to steady profits. For example, a software company that had developed a clearing-house for largent payments might invest in creating hundreds of groups as a means of getting users for its clearing-house services, which would become profitable via a small service fee charged for each transaction.

The Group Structure

The CLIME template for community groups will be familiar to anyone who has served on community committees: the organizers of the group elect a board that is responsible for ensuring the group complies with CLIME's reporting, transparency and governance rules.

The basic requirements of the group template are straightforward *good governance*:

1. The governing board must be elected, and elections must be held at least once a year.
2. Officers are also elected annually: president, treasurer, secretary and membership officer.
3. Proceedings of board meetings are logged and made public to the global CLIME community by the secretary.
4. The treasurer maintains the financial and work records of all group members.
5. The membership officer logs the work record of all members weekly, and make these records public to the global CLIME community. The officer must follow procedures when voiding a membership due to cheating, fraud, misrepresentation, etc., or denying membership to an applicant.
6. A quasi-judicial subcommittee is elected to review any appeals by members who feel their membership was wrongly voided or their work was incorrectly logged.
7. Subcommittees plan and oversee specific work projects. The subcommittee is responsible for ensuring the project follows *best practices* for the region and available labor/capital.

8. Specific work projects are chosen by election in a general meeting.

In addition to the basic requirements for elected leadership, transparency of decision-making, etc., the CLIME system requires that groups accept any applicant who meets their objective standards without regard for the applicant's gender, ethnicity, religion, political views, etc. The objective standards might include a positive peer-to-peer ranking or recommendation by an existing member, and local residency.

Groups are required to serve the needs of a percentage of those in the community who are unable to work: children, the elderly, and those too ill to work. Those who are unable to do certain kinds of work (i.e. the disabled) must be employed by the group in jobs they can perform. Though the percentage of work devoted to caring for those who cannot care for themselves is flexible, each group is required to maintain a permanent work committee to serve local residents who need assistance.

Each group is also required to recruit members to serve on CLIME committees that oversee best practices and governance/compliance issues of the entire system.

In isolated communities, a group might have as few as a dozen members. In urban settings, a successful group might have a thousand or more members, enough to operate a factory, hospital or university.

Those groups that are unable to meet the basic requirements of governance, transparency, membership and work projects will be flagged as needing managerial training. Volunteers from compliant groups will assist in training the struggling group's board, officers and subcommittees.

The global system has two basic features to track group compliance: a technical–assistance program to help groups learn how to meet the requirements, and an audit process to investigate such things as whether a group has failed to complete the work projects it claims to have completed, or is a front for a criminal organization, etc.

As a general rule, the transparency/governance/work requirements are the minimum to ensure the sustainability of the CLIME system. Any group that fails these minimal standards is disqualified. Such failures must be understood as part of the learning process as organizers and members learn from the failures of groups.

The CLIME model, as noted previously, follows a philosophy of *low barriers to entry, high standards of compliance*. In practical terms, this manifests as a systemic philosophy of *fail often, fail fast* as the optimum way to speed learning and spawn successful groups.

The Flexibility of the Group Structure

Even though the CLIME system is at present a theoretical model rather than a living ecosystem, we can anticipate that the great flexibility of the group structure lends itself to experimentation and a spectrum of activities serving communities large and small.

The CLIME system will not restrict members or groups from earning a profit in CLIME or in the outside market. Thus a group might plant a community garden to supply its membership with whatever foodstuffs are scarce, and if this is successful, sell the surplus to other CLIME groups or on the outside marketplace. The only requirements of a group are:

1. The group serves a percentage of the local community that cannot work/care for themselves.
2. The group provides opportunities to contribute for those limited to certain kinds of work.
3. The group democratically selects its work projects.
4. The group accepts largents as payment for goods and services sold within the CLIME system.
5. The group cooperates with other CLIME groups in the larger community via a *Council of Local Groups*.

We can anticipate that some groups will suffer from low productivity, and in these cases the group's primary role may be to provide a market for those within CLIME with surplus to sell.

Some groups with entrepreneurial founders may focus on profitable work projects from the start; others may focus on activities that are not tuned to profits such as child care, education, enhancing the lives of the elderly, etc. We can also imagine groups with several types of complementary work projects. For example, a group might select one project to earn a profit that will subsidize other high-value projects that have little or no profit potential.

How the group reinvests or distributes the profits is decided by the membership. We can easily conceive of a group that is formed to construct housing for its members, and finds that the members develop expertise in that skillset that is marketable to nearby groups. In an urban setting, a group might construct surplus housing units to rent to CLIME members in other groups, or to those outside the system.

Groups founded by those with specific talents may be organized to provide services or training to hundreds or thousands of other CLIME members in other groups. For example, a handful of doctors and nurses might launch a group specifically to fund and staff a multidisciplinary clinic. A core association of educators might form a group with the sole intention of starting and operating a training facility.

The Pareto Principle suggests that roughly 20% of the groups in any region will generate 80% of the surplus goods and services. The most successfully managed groups will attract the most ambitious members, while subpar groups may find that simply meeting the minimal standards is all they can accomplish with the membership and resources at hand.

This disparity is a systemic advantage rather than a problem, as the guaranteed income of members in marginal groups gives even the lowest-productivity groups the means to improve their lives by buying the surplus of more productive groups. The groups that generate large surpluses need markets for their surplus, and lower productivity groups within the system provide this demand.

In other words, the system does not attempt to create groups with equal skills, productivity or work projects. The system is designed to encourage groups to arise wherever there are scarcities and unmet community needs. That some groups will operate much like corporations, while others will operate in more informal, low-key ways is one of the key strengths of the system. If there is a widespread scarcity of healthcare, then a clinic that operates like a corporation might be the most productive solution to the scarcity. If the scarcity is in services for the elderly or childcare, then more informally managed groups will arise to meet those scarcities.

The low barriers to entry and high standards of compliance place a premium on those willing to start a new group, and on those with the skills needed to manage the group to remain compliant.

Groups and members will self-organize according to the local scarcities and the interests and skills of members. A person who realizes they don't like agricultural work might leave that group to join one providing healthcare. A person seeking high-level skills may move to another group as their skills advance. Groups that are successful will create demand for other services, spawning new opportunities for other groups.

For example, the group that launches a successful clinic may find there isn't enough housing for its growing membership. A group that is efficient at building housing may expand to meet that need.

The most important feature of the group structure is that every member of every group is guaranteed a paid job doing something that the group has chosen as valuable to the community. Every member is free to switch groups, work part-time in several groups, work part-time in a group and operate a for-profit household business in their spare time, or start a new group.

The rules governing groups are simple: transparency, good governance, elected leadership, and work projects that serve the community. Beyond these minimal rules, the system self-organizes to best meet local scarcities and make best use of available people and resources.

This self-organizing creates capital as individual members optimize their choices and advance their skills, and as groups fill the most pressing scarcities and compete with other groups for productive members. Groups may fail, and work projects within successful groups may fail. *Fail often, fail fast* generates experimentation, learning and improves best practices.

Organizing Work Flow in the Group

In essence, CLIME organizes and pays underutilized labor to address local scarcities. This matching is unlikely to be perfect. We can anticipate that in many cases, the current interests and skills of the membership will not be prepared for the enormity of local scarcities. But if groups choose work projects that fit the current interests and skills of the members, they might be leaving the most pressing local scarcities unmet.

CLIME requires groups to democratically select the greatest unmet scarcities in their community and devote their efforts to meeting those needs. If the necessary capital and skills are not at hand, the groups must reach out to other groups for best practices templates, training and perhaps even loans to buy needed materials.

Since each group must devote some effort to caring for those in the community who can't care for themselves and have at least one work project, each group has a minimum of two projects. Given that the *Council of Local Groups* is tasked with coordinating the efforts of all local groups, we can anticipate that groups may select more than one work project: one in conjunction with other groups, and one that is solely their own.

How do groups organize the work? How do individuals choose the work they want to do?

One principle of CLIME is that all labor in a group is paid equally to avoid the temptations of privilege. As a result, pay is not a means of prioritizing tasks. (Less productive groups receive lower pay, as discussed below, but the pay within each group is always equal.)

Since CLIME is voluntary, work is not organized around obedience or coercion. Rather, the work flow in groups aims to optimize member choice while getting the work done as efficiently as possible.

Ideally, every task—even the unpleasant ones such as trash collection— is voluntarily filled by a member. But given that some essential work will be difficult and/or unpleasant, there must be a mechanism to assign the unpleasant work in equal proportion to every member—including the leadership.

Fortunately, this process can be performed by unbiased software. For example, if no one volunteers to do trash collection, each member is assigned an hour to two of this work per week.

The way to avoid this duty is to volunteer to do some other kind of work that the membership is avoiding, for example, cleaning animal pens.

This system of assigning essential work that is unfilled by volunteers encourages members to volunteer for whatever unpleasant work they like best, and minimizes the burdens on everyone by requiring a very modest amount of time be spent on work nobody likes.

Work that is more desirable is managed by a matching process: the group's elected leadership prioritizes tasks and members volunteer for the tasks. Members might seek to work with friends, get work that fit their interests, or choose whatever work appears the easiest. (CLIME does not presuppose everyone is a hard-working, industrious saint.)

Individuals who can't find any tasks they're willing to do are free to seek membership in another group, start their own group or leave CLIME for the for-profit sector.

CLIME is like a for-profit enterprise in this way: If you want to get paid, you must perform work the organization needs done.

In general, individuals will be motivated to work for the weekly pay and for the chance to do important work in an atmosphere of group effort.

Groups and Super-Groups

As noted above, the Pareto Principle—a power-law distribution commonly found in Nature—suggests that roughly 20% of the groups in any region will generate 80% of the surplus goods and services. If we explore this further, we can anticipate that 20% of the members in every group will generate 80% of the value and that 20% of the groups may hold 80% of the membership.

This distribution suits CLIME, which is organized to provide a stable income and benefits of membership for all while enabling opportunities to achieve a variety of goals. CLIME is not organized to limit the top 20% but to raise the productivity, income, capital and well-being of all members. If the top 20% are free to boost the income and capital of the group, this boosts the income and capital of the 80% as well.

Some high-achievers may leave CLIME to make their fortunes in the profit-driven sector. Some may see this as a weakness of CLIME, that the most successful members are free to leave the system to seek a private fortune. But this freedom of movement (i.e. agency) is a strength of CLIME, as the free flow of talent, innovation, information and capital benefits each member and the entire system during their membership. Those who leave CLIME for the profit-maximizing sector will act as emissaries and evangelists (assuming they left on good terms) who may well facilitate mutually beneficial trade between CLIME groups and the for-profit sector. Other high-achievers will prefer to stay in CLIME and seek management positions in their group.

Some groups may operate for-profit businesses within CLIME that sell most of their production to those outside CLIME. These groups will naturally attract the most ambitious workers, as the gains from such enterprise will flow to the membership of these groups.

If we combine these elements, we see the potential for *super-groups* to emerge: groups that generate far more output and attract far more members than average groups.

We can also foresee another form of *super-group* in the taxonomy of CLIME groups: an alliance of groups within the global alliance of CLIME.

There are many reasons why groups might form a close alliance. One set of reasons arises from geographic location and proximity. Groups in a destabilized region, for example, might coordinate security for all the CLIME groups in the area. Other reasons arise from shared expertise, markets and interests. Groups that specialize in machining metal parts, for example, might form unique ties as they share tools, techniques and markets for their products.

These networks of groups might operate along the lines of a latter-day Hanseatic League, a model that my colleague Mark Gallmeier believes has much merit for independent groups and super-groups.

Competition is an integral part of CLIME: competition for members, markets and value.

Some groups blessed with particularly effective leadership and deep pools of talent will naturally outperform less well-managed groups, and these highly successful groups will naturally attract the most ambitious members. Such super-groups might have thousands of members while the average group has far fewer members.

Several factors will tend to limit the expansion of super-groups. One is that the expertise to manage 1,000 members may not be sufficient to manage 10,000 members. Another is that rival factions in the group may leave to form a new group, taking a major chunk of the membership with them. A third factor is the characteristics that led people to join the group tend to erode as the group expands.

The alliance super-group may outcompete the single super-group in some settings, while the integrated super-group might outcompete the alliance type in other settings.

We can even foresee an alliance of groups that have chosen to remain small, i.e. with 50 or fewer members, as a way of offsetting the advantages offered by super-groups. Such artisanal groups may choose to remain small, while other groups may have to scale up as the only way to address the scarcities in their community.

Certain tasks lend themselves to super-groups. For example, a large clinic-hospital requires a level of management and expertise that is best served by some form of super-group.

Other tasks might require a temporary super-group. If a regional *Council of Local Groups* (see below) decided that a new bridge would serve all CLIME groups in the area, the groups might form an alliance with the sole task of building the bridge. Once the project is completed, the groups would dissolve this single-project alliance.

Very large-scale projects may require global super-groups to assemble the necessary capital, expertise and materials.

CLIME enables and encourages an almost infinite variety of groups, all arising from the variables of specific geographies, cultures, interests and needs.

The Council of Local Groups

CLIME has one formal super-group: the *Council of Local Groups.* Every group must join a *Council of Local Groups* that coordinates local efforts on problems that cannot be effectively solved by any one group:

medical care, mental health, care of the elderly, childcare, homelessness, food security, and so on. The Council of Local Groups structure enables coordinated effort and sharing of what works best in particular circumstances with other Councils globally.

As note previously, every group is required to devote a significant percentage of its labor and capital to caring for those who cannot care for themselves. The Council structure enables local groups to tackle problems that require sustained, coordinated effort—for example, improving water quality for the entire city/area.

The Council structure provides a means of organizing the work force of the entire region. We can anticipate that Councils of Councils will arise to coordinate regional solutions, with the understanding that the Council of Councils has no authority within CLIME. Just as the individual can always opt in or out of a CLIME group, a Council of Councils is voluntary: it arises to better serve a regional need, not to exercise centralized power.

CLIME Has No Centralized Leadership

While the CLIME software is managed and maintained by a non-profit board, the system has no centralized leadership. In terms of operational direction and choice, CLIME is a system of local and *emergent leadership*, meaning leaders arise every time a new group is established or a new slate of leaders is elected in an existing group.

How the system expands in any specific region or nation depends not on a centralized authority pushing orders down a hierarchy, but instead on the choices of individual members and the leaders they democratically select within groups. As a result, we can anticipate a great diversity of CLIME groups, alliances and priorities within regions. Some areas may quickly establish formal alliances between groups (i.e. super-groups) or scale up using the best available technologies. Groups in other regions may choose to remain small and fiercely independent.

This reliance on emergent leadership is a key strength of CLIME. The system thrives on *diversity, the free flow of information, choice and feedback*, and rejects centralization and hierarchy as organizing principles.

Why Start a CLIME Group?

Why would an individual start a CLIME group? There are three basic motivations:

1. The individual has no income (or no reliable income) and wants a secure income.
2. The individual is tired of being unproductive and wants to be useful and productive.
3. The individual sees scarcities/unmet needs in his/her community and wants to address them.

There are also additional potential motivators:

1. The individual is lonely and wants a reliable, trustworthy social circle.
2. To borrow Steve Jobs' phrase, the individual has a burning desire to do something *insanely great* and CLIME offers a complete package to do so: capital, connections and labor.

CLIME Groups' Unique Role in the Community Economy

What does a CLIME group do that the profit-maximizing market and the state can't do? Why do we need the CLIME system at all?

The first answer is that the current systems are incapable of creating jobs for everyone who wants one.

The second answer is: *CLIME groups do all the work that profit-maximizing enterprises and the state cannot do or have no interest in doing.* Though the current narrative assumes that all work worth doing is performed for a profit or by the state, as we have seen in the examples of bikeways and near-zero cost education, there are enormous swaths of work that are useful and necessary that do not generate a profit nor do they lend themselves to the costly, privilege-protecting hierarchies of the state.

The truth is that only a very narrow slice of the human experience can be served at a profit. If we remove the blinders of the state and its handmaiden, consumerism, we can see vast vistas of work that are intrinsically unprofitable and beyond the scope of the state.

CLIME groups play another vital role: *they offer competition to the monopolies of the state and profit-maximizing enterprises*. As noted in Section 1, monopoly is the ideal way to maximize profits and protect privileges. In effect, the state's *raison d'etre* (reason to exist) is to monopolize power and the issuance of money and credit, which gives it monopoly control of wealth. Profit-maximizing enterprises carve out a monopoly under the wing of the state.

CLIME groups are free to assess the greatest scarcities in their community and alleviate those scarcities. If those scarcities are the result of state-cartel monopolies, CLIME groups may begin producing whatever goods and services are scarce, in direct competition with the monopoly.

Monopolies will naturally fiercely resist this competition, but several systemic factors complicate their suppression of competition.

1. They cannot control the CLIME currency or network. They can attempt to ban it, but since it resides in ubiquitous devices and networks (smart phones and the web), it is essentially impossible to eliminate it.
2. CLIME operates at the lowest levels of the economy, It is in effect a global black market with its own currency and network of production and distribution. History shows us that the more oppressive the monopoly, the more pervasive and effective the black market.
3. The political and financial power of the global CLIME community.

The Political and Financial Influence of the Global CLIME Community

When the CLIME system launches, the number of groups will be small. But as the failures of the current world-system spread like a firestorm across the global economy, we can anticipate the equally rapid spread of CLIME.

The Pareto Principle informs this expansion of CLIME. The 80/20 distribution can be distilled down to 4/64, as the top 20% of the 20% have an outsized influence on 80% of the 80%. Once 4% of the global economy has a CLIME presence, we can anticipate a very rapid expansion to 64% of the global economy.

The dominant financial and political powers—currently America, the European Union, Japan and China--will likely resist the global spread of a non-state system that is outside their control. But as the failures of the current world system consume the periphery economies (often called *emerging market economies*), the crises will spread from the periphery to the core developed nations.

Developed economies that have not yet lost their local community economies will be unable to limit the emergence of CLIME in these local communities, which lack what CLIME generates from its first week of operation: cash income for all, a market for their production and a source of capital.

Once the CLIME system scales up to 10 million members (roughly the size of a megalopolis city), the unified actions of the members will exert a global influence. This action might take the form of a publicity campaign that documents the repression of CLIME groups by a particular nation-state, or it might take the form of a boycott of a global corporation that has sought to repress the competition of CLIME groups. This unified action is ultimately motivated by the self-interest of each member and each group, since the potential wealth CLIME generates for each member ad group increases as more people and groups join CLIME.

The larger the market, the more goods and services can be sold. As productive people join the system, the sum of knowledge and expertise available to all expands. And as the number of members drawing wages expands, so does the purchasing power and capital of the entire system.

Once CLIME has 50 million members—the equivalent of a major nation-state, but still less than 1% of the total human population of around 7.4 billion—the political and economic power of the global memberships' unified actions will rival that of nation-states. This global reach will play an important role in breaking down repressive regimes, monopolies, and protected privileges, one at a time, everywhere that CLIME arises to provide paid work and alleviate poverty.

CLIME Eliminates Exploitation of Labor

The exploitation of labor—paying very low wages, cheating employees of their pay, and so on—is only possible when paid work is scarce and the number of unemployed people is high. By guaranteeing wages to everyone who wants a job, CLIME establishes a base minimum wage that other employers (the state and profit-maximizing enterprises) will have to match, and a minimum standard for treatment of workers. If an individual can quit the state or private employer and join a CLIME group at will, their ex-employers will be forced to match or exceed the pay and other benefits offered by CLIME groups. As a result, CLIME raises the standard of living of all employees, not just the wages of people who join a CLIME group.

The Power of Peers

Research has found that individual goals such as losing weight, becoming more fit, managing anxiety disorders, etc. are typically best served by groups of peers with the same goals. To keep on track, each group is managed by a trained person. The support of peers in a goal-oriented structure helps individuals deal with the challenges and setbacks that are part of the process.

The group structure of CLIME lends itself very naturally to the formation of support groups designed to help individuals reach their own health/career/personal goals, and to the training of group leaders according to best practices.

The Power of CLIME Data

Identifying, codifying and improving best practices for a variety of circumstances is a critical step in improving productivity and *doing more with less*. The CLIME system enables and encourages this process on a global scale, as every group is required to track the labor, capital and resources devoted to each work project and log the results. This data (stripped of individual identities to protect privacy) is available to everyone in the CLIME system for analysis. Rather than guessing what works best in a specific setting, everyone within CLIME will have access to data-based results on what worked or didn't work elsewhere in the system.

This vast trove of data will speed the process of identifying and refining best practices for specific settings of geography, resource constraints, cultural issues, etc.

CLIME Relocalizes Work and Wealth

One of the historical consequences of a lack of paid work is migration of the unemployed to more prosperous nations. This migration tends to bleed the impoverished regions of talent and capital, while generating conflict in the magnet regions.

The purpose of CLIME is to create paid work everywhere on the planet for anyone who wants it. People may still choose to migrate to better or different opportunities elsewhere, but with CLIME, anyone who wants paid work need only start or join a CLIME group where they live. In CLIME, there is no need to relocate to find paid work. Paid work is available in every community, nation and region once a single individual starts a CLIME group.

CLIME doesn't just provide paid work. It also builds capital, which is the engine of wealth creation. CLIME relocalizes paid work and wealth by generating a global network of markets, capital and expertise.

CLIME Addresses Intractable Problems For-Profit Enterprises and the State Fail to Solve

As noted earlier, CLIME empowers the community economy to address problems that are not profitable or optimized for state hierarchies—for example, homelessness and the related issues of mental health, housing, and drug abuse. Research has found that group engagement is the essential foundation of long-term solutions to these related problems, and CLIME offers the labor pool, capital, shared data and resources needed to assemble and sustain group-based solutions to problems that are intractable in the current world system.

CLIME Reflects the Messiness of Innovation and Adaptation

Given the newness of CLIME's systems and its demands on the individual, we can anticipate a very high failure rate of groups, individuals and systems in the initial stages. Some people will find the technology of establishing a group too daunting; others will fail to file the required reports and will lose their group accreditation. Still others will attempt to cheat the system, get caught and have their membership revoked. Evil hackers will try to create millions of counterfeit largents for their own use, and various bugs in the software will, as always, be discovered at the least convenient moments.

All of this is to be expected. People will naturally test the system to see if they can establish a privilege or free-ride off others' labor. The automated software will have to be good enough to catch the majority of these cheats and frauds and revoke their membership.

But even beyond this initial phase of testing and learning how the system functions, CLIME will still be semi-chaotic and messy. CLIME is an intrinsically messy system, optimized for wide-open experimentation within the code of conduct of equal treatment of all members and groups. The CLIME structure optimizes *agency, freedom of movement* and *choice*. Once members grasp this great freedom, they will naturally check out a variety of groups, and some will establish their own group to bypass the problems they see in existing groups.

All of this is healthy; this churn is the cost of freedom and innovation.

- If a system is stripped of redundancy, it becomes inherently fragile.
- If a system is stripped of choice and the resulting churn, it is stripped of freedom and innovation.

CLIME is robust enough to bear the inevitable costs of this constant churn of members and groups.

There is no other way to provide authentic agency and freedom of movement. There will always be members switching groups, starting new groups, recruiting members from existing groups, quitting in disgust if their faction loses an election, and people whose membership has been revoked for breaking the rules of conduct who claim they were wronged. Some people may flit endlessly between groups, doing very little productive work. Others may be serial group-starters, launching one group after another and then quitting them shortly thereafter. Some people may stay in the same group their entire membership. Others might switch back and forth between CLIME membership and for-profit enterprises.

Some groups might expend much of their energy on infighting. Others will grow quickly, do great work and then fade. Individual and group dynamics have free rein in CLIME, and this will naturally create many frustrations for those trying to get productive work done. But the freedom of movement means those frustrated with dysfunctional or low-productivity groups can leave and start their own group, with higher standards for work performance.

The messiness of CLIME reflects the intrinsic messiness of experimentation, adaptation and innovation. This messiness is the engine that keeps CLIME dynamic, adaptable, innovative and stable.

The one solid foundation that anchors the system is very simple: regardless of any other conditions, everyone who does accredited work in an accredited group gets paid at the end of the work week.

Enforcing Bias-Free Self-Organizing Groups

People often feel more comfortable with others of their own class (however we define *class*) and so we can anticipate that many groups will be largely homogenous. The CLIME system requires every group to accept members who meet their publicly posted requirements, with the caveat that groups can accept a limited number of new members at a time, as the management of the group must expand along with the membership. Some groups may choose to remain small, and the system does not force groups to expand.

The system must self-monitor bias to avoid becoming a system of haves and have-nots in which *some are more equal than others*. But the system does not enforce quotas; it only requires members be accepted on transparent, objective qualifications that have nothing to do with ethnicity, religion, political views or gender.

However, we must recognize that following formal rules of membership does not mean members are required to socialize with each other. We can imagine a group formed around a specific religious faith who must accept an avowed atheist against the groups' unspoken wishes for a fellowship restricted to those of their own faith. The atheist may be a member in a formal sense, but the other members may shun him/her socially. The solution to the issue of informal bias in the CLIME system is to start a new group with members that share similar desires for diversity of community.

The CLIME system is not intended to suppress or champion any cultural value system other than the basic human rights of free association and membership rules that are free of ethnic, religious, political or gender bias.

Self-organized groups are inherently non-hierarchical. Those violating the basic rules of the system lose their accreditation. Beyond this, it is up to each member to choose a group or start a group that functions not just according to the CLIME system's rules but in a manner that makes the member comfortable with his/her membership.

The Process of Verifying Compliance and Work

As noted in previous sections, the integrity of the CLIME system requires a rigorous protocol of verifying that the work that groups claim was done was indeed done. I have phrased the philosophy guiding the protocols as *the barriers to entry are low, but the barriers to fraud are high*, and *low barriers to entry, high standards of compliance*.

The key mechanism of verifying compliance is automated review by fraud-detection software, and randomized peer-to-peer review by members in other groups.

Members who volunteer (or are assigned by their group) to check on other groups' work projects receive appropriate training and are paid just as if they were working on a project within their group.

The group itself receives a small bonus payment for every member who serves the larger CLIME community by performing audit/verification duties.

Members and groups who uncover fraud/theft/misrepresentation receive an additional bonus payment. This motivates detective work into suspicious circumstances within groups. (The identity of auditors and their groups is confidential so they remain anonymous to those being audited).

To avoid false claims of fraud as a means of collecting the bonus, those submitting claims of fraud that cannot be substantiated are flagged;

repeated reports of fraud that are not substantiated trigger removal of those members from oversight duties.

The field of fraud detection is well-developed, and those processes can be applied to the automated scan of work records. The automated fraud detection software looks for signs that claims are fraudulent by comparing properly verified work projects with new claims. Projects that drag on long past the typical completion date, for example, would be flagged, as would a project that looks suspiciously like a mansion being constructed for a criminal leader.

Did the work actually get done? Fraud detection software randomly selects members from the global community to investigate flagged claims. Preference is given to volunteers in the physical vicinity of the suspicious claim who can visit the group's work site, but satellite/drone imagery and other tools enable remote assessment by volunteers far from the actual site.

The CLIME system is based on a simple core rule: *only verified work is paid*. This is different from *all work is paid and then verified*. Only work progress that has been verified by peer-to-peer review or evidence such as before-and-after satellite/drone imagery gets paid. If the work claim has been flagged as suspicious, the system automatically assigns randomly selected volunteers to review the evidence. (Mathematically speaking, a completely random selection is not possible, so the system makes an approximation of random selection.)

Each week's work progress is reviewed by a new randomly selected reviewer.

The point here is that the randomized selection of review members and the weekly cycling of reviewers makes it impossible for a corrupt group to game the system by bribing the reviewers. The group being reviewed does not know the identity of the reviewers or the means being used to verify their work claims.

Since any work that has been flagged as suspicious cannot be paid, those performing the work are incentivized to be accurate and transparent in their work claims so they will get paid.

In addition, the automated fraud detection software randomly selects work projects to be audited by CLIME audit teams, both on the ground and using technological verification means. This randomized audit process greatly incentivizes compliance, because no member or group can be sure that their false claim won't be flagged by the automated software or uncovered in a random audit.

High audit rates increase incentives for compliance. For this reason, a high rate of randomized audits is the default system setting—perhaps as high as 50% of all work claims in groups that have yet to establish their reliability and integrity and 5% of all work claims in established groups.

The process of auditing means that every group needs other trustworthy groups to verify its work claims, even as groups might be competing for members. Groups with extremely high compliance ratings become desirable to members, as these groups are less likely to have their work records flagged and their payments withheld.

If a group files a suspicious work claim, payments to the entire membership of the group (and to the group itself) are withheld, pending resolution of the audit. If a group has three projects in progress and one is flagged, pay on all three projects is withheld. This creates peer pressure on all members and work projects to comply transparently and accurately, as even one member who attempts to fudge their work claim will cause everyone in the group to not get paid.

A new group might get flagged repeatedly for failing to properly log their work progress. This delayed payment for work completed incentivizes every member in a group to be scrupulous about accurately reporting not just their own work but the work of others, as anyone who attempts to fudge their own reports ends up penalizing the entire group.

(As a practical matter, work records are logged from Wednesday to Tuesday, leaving three days for the work progress to be verified so payments can be issued on Friday afternoon.)

This system is designed so it's *easy to comply, and difficult to cheat.* Members will note that their work project has been audited on a regular basis, and that the audit process is opaque to those being audited. It's much easier to simply comply, as the cost of triggering an audit to the group is very high and the potential gains so paltry.

The fraud detection system is also directed at all software to ensure the software hasn't been modified to benefit the few at the expense of the many. Anyone detecting irregularities in the software is paid a bonus, as anyone uncovering fraud in the system receives a bonus.

Human nature is highly attuned to fairness and injustice. People who have to work for their wage resent those who are getting paid while avoiding work. The system enables members who see others committing fraud to report the injustice via SMS or email messages to the fraud-detection system. These reports are kept anonymous so whistleblowers cannot be punished by thieves and cheats.

This automated fraud detection and randomized audit process is expensive but essential to maintain the integrity of the CLIME system globally. If the fraud-detection and audit process are 10% of the total system costs, the system issues the money to pay these costs directly to the system's software engineers and members in the randomly selected audit teams.

The Peer-to-Peer Trust Ranking System

Many of us are familiar with the customer reviews on Yelp and similar peer-to-peer ranking websites. The problem with these sites is the reviewers are not rated, so we have no way of assessing the integrity of their review.

The CLIME peer-to-peer software engine generates an objective form of *social capital for each member* by ranking each member's history of accuracy/integrity. The verifications provided by those who have earned high rankings are given more weight than verifications provided by new members or those with low rankings.

Each report by a member is rated against other evidence for accuracy. Members who accurately report their work project's progress and those of other projects receive high rankings. Members whose reports are at odds with other accounts, satellite imagery, etc. are ranked lower, as are reports that are ambiguous when others are definitive or definitive when the evidence is ambiguous.

This system offers a number of advantages to members, groups and the global CLIME system.

Members with high rankings will be trusted throughout the system, and will thus be in higher demand than those with poor rankings.

The reports of members with high rankings carry more weight when verifying other's integrity, so these members are in demand by others seeking accreditation of accuracy, skills, trustworthiness, etc.

A member's ranking increases when he/she:

1. Accurately reports the work progress of their own project and the projects of others.
2. Accurately reports the decision-making process in a group, the audit trail pursued by an audit team, etc.
3. Accurately verifies the skills and integrity of another member.

Members who act as *mentors* to junior members will typically have high rankings, as will *super-users*—those members who belong to numerous groups within CLIME. *Super-users* are *go-to people*—the individuals others seek out for advice or for suggestions on how to get a job done.

The value of a high ranking incentivizes being careful with what and whom one accredits. If a member is caught misrepresenting a work report, for example, it's not just his/her ranking that suffers—everyone who verified that person as trustworthy also suffers a decline in their ranking. This makes it difficult for a scammer to acquire accreditation from highly trustworthy members, as those with high ranking earned those rankings by being scrupulous in their reporting. They have no incentive to issue a positive report on a complete stranger, as their own ranking will drop precipitously if that person turns out to be a scammer.

If a criminal group attempts to coerce those with high rankings to verify their work, an anonymous message from those being pressured will immediately freeze the largent assets of the criminal group, pending a detailed audit by randomly selected auditors from the global CLIME system.

New members who make false claims on behalf of friends and cronies will receive a ranking of zero—untrustworthy. No group is required to accept members who have proven to be untrustworthy.

Filing false reports to benefit oneself or a crony yields very limited results, as every report by every member is cross-checked against other reports and evidence by the automated peer-to-peer ranking engine. A false or misleading report cannot possibly yield any payoff unless it is supported by a host of other false reports, and this network of falsity increases the chances of the system identifying discrepancies with factual evidence. As a result, falsifying or exaggerating reports fails to yield much of a benefit while the cost of the false report is very high, as the membership of the untrustworthy is voided and they will be avoided by other CLIME groups.

Given that the audit process pursues every source of verifiable evidence and every report by members, the opportunities to file false claims and remain undiscovered are very slim. False reports will immediately be flagged by the audit-detection software as not matching other evidence. Should a member's claim be verified as false, their ranking of integrity and trustworthiness falls to zero. The number of groups willing to entrust a person who has falsified reports to serve their own greed at the expense of the group is near-zero. Scammers who attempt to game the system by falsifying reports effectively choose pariah status. By attempting to cheat the system, they have chosen not to participate in CLIME.

Best Practices: Sustainable, Efficient and Productive

One of the core requirements of all CLIME groups is that they use *best practices and appropriate technologies* in all work projects. Insisting on best practices and appropriate technologies is designed to extract the most productivity from the labor, resources and capital being invested in the project. The goal of best practices is *sustainable productivity and faster, better, cheaper.*

Exploiting resources is not sustainable, and low productivity activities waste resources, capital and labor. Every work project should strive to use the least amount of resources, labor and capital and be faster, better and cheaper than other options.

Technology typically imposes trade-offs in cost, capital and resources needed to complete the project. The solution is to seek the most appropriate technologies for the climate and community performing the work. In general, the most appropriate technologies are those that the participants can construct themselves out of cheap, easily obtainable materials, and that are powered by renewable energy sources.

Establishing the *best practices and appropriate technologies* for a specific community can be ascertained by asking this question: given our specific circumstances, what have others found to be the optimum solutions in terms of cost, efficiency, sustainability and minimal use of resources?

One example of an appropriate technology is the bicycle. While those enamored of high-technology envision self-driving electric vehicles with horrendously costly (and at present unsustainable) battery packs, the majority of communities are better served (depending on the climate and topography) with human-power/semi-powered cycles that can be repaired locally and whose metal components last for years or even decades. In other words, appropriate technology is not just a matter of wealth or poverty; it is a global metric of efficient use of resources, sustainability and the well-being of communities and individuals.

 This requirement to employ best practices and the most appropriate technologies has two purposes:

1. Making best use of labor, resources, knowledge and technologies.
2. Establishing a global benchmark that cannot be gamed to benefit the few at the expense of the many.

Imagine a criminal gang that threatens a group unless they build the gang's leader a mansion. If there were no limitations on a group's selection of a work project, this coerced choice might escape detection. But since all proposed work projects must pass the test of best practices, it is highly unlikely that a poor village's proposed plan to build a mansion that cannot possibly serve the village's most pressing scarcities would be approved. The warlord might enslave the villagers to build his mansion, but the CLIME system cannot be hijacked to serve the warlord.

The bias in favor of traditional methods often conflicts with an equally adamant bias in favor of new technologies. From the point of view of best practices and appropriate technologies, neither is automatically the best choice for a community. Traditional practices have limitations, especially if they are practiced without care being given to productivity and sustainability, and technologies that are costly and difficult to maintain are equally limited in applicability.

Best practices and appropriate technologies are key forms of human and intellectual capital. Distributing these forms of capital to every CLIME group is an essential step in building the wealth-producing capital of households and communities.

Best practices also encompass the managing of groups and work projects. Learning the best practices of managing work projects is a valuable form of human capital that generates wealth for individuals, groups and communities.

Best practices are also about making work easier and more humane. Since the motive isn't profit but *doing more with less*, models of low-impact sustainability that free people from drudgery become the best practices globally.

The Largent Money System

The conceptual core of the largent money system is that money is a mechanism for trading surpluses of goods and services for cash that can be used to buy something that is desirable/scarce. The largent alleviates poverty by distributing money directly to those who are creating goods and services in their community. To the degree that poverty is a nexus of needs that cannot be filled due to lack of paid work, a labor-backed currency is the only possible solution that provides paid work, mechanisms to build capital and needed goods and services in communities. A labor-backed currency is the only system that resolves the crises of employment, purpose, community, sustainability and poverty in one integrated solution.

The CLIME/Largent Model: A Membership Organization That Pays Wages in Largents

Technically speaking, the CLIME system is not a currency issuer, nor is it a bank. CLIME is (for lack of a better phrase) a *Membership Organization* comprised of every member who joins an accredited community group. CLIME pays its members in largents, and maintains digital accounts for its members so they can conduct financial transactions in largents. It only issues largents to its members as wages or earned bonuses for auditing work.

CLIME is not a bank. It does not open accounts for non-members, nor does it issue credit or loans. As a result, CLIME and the largent are not under the purview of banking or currency-issuance laws.

The CLIME/largent model is not a conventional employee/employer relationship; it is a new model, and thus a *new form of symbolic capital*. Only accredited members of accredited community groups receive largents in exchange for verified work. But the members are not directly employed by CLIME; they are *members* of a community group they freely join or leave. One of the requirements of membership is accepting largents as payment in full for one's labor.

This model does not align with conventional currencies and banks, and thus is outside currency/ banking regulations. Any attempt by authorities to impose currency/banking regulations on CLIME will be rejected as inapplicable. Since CLIME and largent data are encrypted and distributed, authorities will find it difficult to locate whatever it is they claim falls under their regulation.

One foundational principle of the CLIME/largent system is that it is not beholden to any corporation or state for its operations. CLIME needs no one's approval to operate globally.

Pricing Wages in Largents Locally and Globally

How much is a largent worth? How many largents are paid for a day's labor? The general answer is that largents are priced dynamically by supply and demand. But the system must have some basis for deciding how many largents will be issued in each community for a day's labor.

While the simple solution would be to issue one sum of largents for a day's labor everywhere in the world, this fails to account for the highly variable cost of living.

One practical way to price largents globally is to gather the cost of a basket of necessities in each CLIME region, for example, the cost of 1,000 calories of locally abundant foods, 1 BTU of energy and one square meter of living space. The cost of these necessities would be priced in global currencies such as the U.S. dollar, local currencies and gold to reach a price that makes sense locally and globally.

In regions where these necessities are expensive, members will be paid more largents than those members in areas with low costs of the same necessities.

Since CLIME is a global system, such variability is built into the system. As soon as largents are distributed widely, a market will arise to trade largents for other currencies, commodities, precious metals and indeed, everything that is currently traded globally.

In effect, the largent must be priced dynamically to reflect the global differences in costs of necessities and the value of the goods and services being produced by each group. The software that issues and distributes largents must track regional prices of a basket of necessities and adjust wages to reflect changes in the market.

This is similar to the function of the MIT Billion Price Project. CLIME's automated price/value data collection software also generates a relative measure of price inflation/deflation in the largent universe.

What the system is pricing regionally is the *purchasing power of labor*. In general, the goal is to set the value of labor in largents at a level that enables every household enough income to buy the necessities locally *within the CLIME system* and have some disposable income left for savings or other discretionary purchases.

We can anticipate that everyone earning largents will feel they should be paid more. The system ideal is that someone currently earning 100 largents in their community could move to another locale where the pay is 200 largents, and they would find their higher pay buys about the same necessities as their 100 largents did back home.

By tracking the real-time market for labor, goods and services, the system dynamically adjusts the largents being paid to align with the costs of essentials in each community.

The goal of the CLIME system is that scarcities that generate high prices locally will be met with increased production or substitutions elsewhere in the CLIME system.

The system's automated dynamic pricing also seeks to maintain the purchasing power of largents by aligning wages to the value of the goods and services being produced by each group. Groups with low productivity receive lower pay. This dynamic pricing of output ensures that those who choose to work unproductively will not receive the same compensation as those who are working productively.

Over time, groups that ineffectively manage their members' labor will disband as members abandon those groups in favor of more productive groups earning higher wages. This *creative destruction* of poorly managed groups in favor of more productive groups is an essential feature of the CLIME system, as the only sustainable way to increase wealth is by increasing the capital and productivity of members and groups.

Subsidizing unproductive groups by paying them in excess of the value they are creating would effectively lower the purchasing power of the largent globally, hurting every member in the system. The best way to increase the productivity and wealth of members globally is to protect the purchasing power of the largent.

This dynamic pricing cannot possibly meet every goal perfectly, but the system must maintain the purchasing power of the largent and avoid imbalances that reward the unproductive and punish the productive within the system.

The CLIME Clearing-House Provides Basic Banking without Being a Bank

The for-profit banking sector performs several functions which the CLIME system serves with separate systems. The CLIME clearing-house (one of the five software engines of the system) functions as a bank in terms of maintaining accounts for each member and enabling digital credits and payment transactions. Ideally, competing for-profit clearing-houses will arise, each funded by a small fee for each transaction.

The clearing-houses cannot issue loans, but they can issue debit cards linked to member accounts and make foreign-exchange transactions between largents and other currencies. There is nothing in the CLIME system that precludes existing banks or credit unions from offering clearing-house services to CLIME members, provided they establish the CLIME clearing-house services as a separate entity with its own management and books. The CLIME system's management board has the power to solicit competing clearing-house services or ban a service that is deemed exploitive or dishonest.

Peer-to-Peer Lending

Peer-to-peer borrowing and lending largents between groups and members is encouraged in the CLIME system. Groups are not allowed to borrow in other currencies or speculate in stocks, bonds currencies, derivatives, options or commodities. Groups may borrow largents from other groups, and members can borrow from other members or from groups. Largents cannot be loaned to non-members or entities outside the CLIME system.

Fractional reserve lending is prohibited in the CLIME system. Largents cannot be lent into existence. Largents that have been saved from wages can be loaned or given to others.

Loans have a maximum term of one year, to encourage short-term loans and discourage accumulations of debt that exceed members' ability to service their debt.

The interest rate is limited to 5% plus the global inflation rate of the largent, which is calculated monthly by the system's price data collection program. The peer-to-peer lending market is part of the global CLIME marketplace for goods and services; offers to lend largents are transparent to all members.

The CLIME system enables peer-to-peer lending for productive investments, not for speculation. Individual members can transfer their largents into other currencies and speculate with those funds, but the CLIME system prohibits speculating in largents.

We can anticipate informal gambling and small-scale speculation will arise as a manifestation of human nature. The CLIME system has no enforcement mechanism against private, informal gambling and speculation in largents; it simply does not enable it systemically.

Detecting Irregularities in Largent Accounts

As with all CLIME systems, a robust fraud-detection software system monitors largent accounts globally to detect irregularities that could be manifestations of fraud or illegal transactions.

The key tool is *scale*: in a system of many small transactions of small amounts, large transactions, large numbers of transfers and large numbers of coordinated withdrawals are flagged and frozen.

If typical members are paid 100 largents a week, accounts that suddenly hold 10,000 largents will immediately be flagged for investigation and frozen pending the conclusion of the audit.

Since each largent has a unique code, each unit of currency is traceable through every transaction.

How could one member accumulate thousands of largents in a short period of time? One possibility is a criminal gang forced members to transfer funds to its leader. Another is a fraud that persuaded members to transfer funds to the schemer's account.

Since the largent software automatically monitors every account and every transaction, accounts with irregularities are frozen immediately. Should criminals manage to buy goods with stolen largents before their account can be frozen, the system can (upon conclusion of the audit process) reverse those purchases and return the stolen largents to their owners.

Those committing frauds or theft are banned from the CLIME system, and the system solicits photos of the perpetrators from victims to be distributed globally, to minimize opportunities for criminals to re-enter the system with a new identity.

Those members who transferred funds to others in "too good to be true" get-rich-quick schemes will not get their largents back. Those who were coerced by force to transfer their money to thieves will have their largents restored to their accounts.

In general, the system has a low threshold for freezing transactions and accounts. Any irregularity results in a frozen account and an audit, on the philosophy that legitimate transactions must be protected at all costs, and criminal or fraudulent transactions must be deleted or reversed, even at the cost of some convenience to the system at large.

The largent monitoring system is designed on the expectation that a small percentage of members will attempt to exploit the system via theft or fraud. The system's ability to trace every transaction and erase fraudulently obtained largents gives it considerable power to identify and freeze irregularities before the perpetrators can use their ill-gotten largents, and delete/destroy the money as a last resort.

This strict monitoring establishes a powerful self-reinforcing feedback loop as the low returns on criminality and the severe punishment deter those tempted to commit fraud.

The largent system itself must be monitored for software-based fraud, and the most effective way to ensure system integrity is for independent monitoring systems to scan the core system for insider fraud and software vulnerabilities that can be exploited by criminals.

The battle against criminality and fraud is never-ending, and the solution is to devote sufficient resources to monitor and immediately freeze every irregular account and transaction and resolve vulnerabilities via third-party monitoring.

Two key characteristics of the largent system place strict limits on fraud. One is the traceability of each largent, and the second is the small size of transactions and the relatively small number of legitimate transactions in legitimate groups and member accounts. Any transactions above a few hundred largents will be flagged and audited, as will accounts that suddenly log dozens of transactions of any size. The vast majority of these transactions will be legitimate, but the system automatically freezing all large transactions and accounts logging multiple transactions limits thieves and embezzlers to a very narrow straw.

The third limiting characteristic is the system's ability to reverse any transaction deemed illegal and erase any largents obtained illegally. Not only is it difficult to steal or embezzle more than a few largents at a time, it is difficult to steal from hundreds of accounts at the same time. Even if a thief managed to accumulate a large horde of largents, the theft is still not successful because that money will be frozen or erased.

If a criminal manages to buy something with stolen largents, the money will be erased from the seller's accounts, causing the seller to demand payment in legitimate largents or the return of the goods.

Since largents are digital, there is no way to convert them to cash except in other currencies. And since the system monitors foreign-exchange transactions, any thief will not be able to convert large sums of largents into other currencies without the transaction being flagged and frozen before it can even be completed.

As those in law enforcement know, it is impossible to stop all theft and embezzlement. But what is possible is to harden the system so that thieves and embezzlers choose to ply their trade elsewhere.

Why Would Those Outside CLIME Accept Largents?

Why would anyone in the world outside CLIME accept largents for payment? An example illustrates the motive: exchanging surplus goods and services that would otherwise remain unsold.

Let's imagine I have a permanent stand at a farmer's market. By the end of the day, whatever produce I still have on hand has lost its freshness and I will have to dump it in the recycling bin.

A customer comes along and asks if he can pay in largents for the aging produce. He explains that it only takes a moment to set up an account to accept his digital payment. I ask the obvious question: what can I buy with the largents I get? The customer opens the CLIME global marketplace on his smartphone and shows me what's currently for sale—hundreds of goods and services. At this point, I have nothing to lose by selling the surplus inventory that has zero value for me and everything to gain by accepting largents for what would otherwise be worthless produce.

After I close up shop for the day, I look online and discover the largent is trading at about a 20% discount to the U.S. dollar. If I charge 30% more for largent-paying customers, I net an additional 10% profit. After I successfully turn my digital largents into goods I wanted to buy anyway, I start allotting 10% of my business to largent customers.

When one of my suppliers bemoans his inability to sell a shipment of artisan honey because the price can't compete with lower-cost commercial honey, I ask if he'd be willing to accept a 15% premium in largents. I then explain the largent system and CLIME global marketplace, and invite him to check it out online.

Since he can't sell the shipment through normal channels except at a big loss, he accepts my offer and I list the honey on the CLIME marketplace at a 40% premium so I net 25% profit for handling the sales and shipping to largent customers.

For largent customers, my product might be the only locally available honey that can be bought with largents at the moment and I will sell the entire shipment. If there is competing honey available for less, I will have to lower my price in largents to sell the stock.

When a CLIME group offers to buy the entire shipment at a 25% premium, I accept the offer even though my profit drops to 10%, simply to avoid the extra expense of filling smaller orders.

When a produce supplier bemoans his inability to turn a profit due to the saturated market, I suggest expanding into the largent market as a way of maximizing his return. I hear later that he hired an employee with the stipulation that the new employee would only be paid in largents collected from sales on the CLIME marketplace.

In an economy of stagnating wages and profits and rising taxes, the CLIME market offers a rare opportunity to expand profitable sales by selling what was otherwise surplus inventory. This incentive to sell what is otherwise low-value inventory applies to thousands of small businesses, and this market in largent-priced goods enables those who sell goods and services for largents to spend their largents in a global marketplace.

As noted previously, a foreign-exchange market will naturally arise so largents can be traded for other currencies. This exchange rate and the prices for goods and services offered on the CLIME marketplace will naturally create opportunities for arbitrage: canny traders will buy goods priced in largents that are trading at a discount to the foreign-exchange value of largents.

All of this trading generates demand for largents and creates an expanding market for goods and services priced in largents.

Businesses with no employees (i.e. sole proprietors/self-employed) generate about $1 trillion annually in the U.S. alone. Though this is not that large compared to the $17 trillion U.S. economy, it is more than the gross domestic products of many small nations. Self-employed entrepreneurs are by definition open to opportunities that corporations ignore. What percentage of this $1 trillion annually would be enough to create a global marketplace for goods and services priced in largents?

What if we add in all the other sole proprietors /self-employed entrepreneurs in the world? What percentage of their vast business would be enough to generate a network effect for goods and services priced in largents? I think we can conservatively estimate that the percentage needed would be quite low.

Why Would Anyone Sell Gold for Largents?

Skeptics of the largent currency might ask why anyone would be willing to trade gold for largents. After all, the largent is a digital currency that isn't backed by anything other than demand while gold is a timeless store of value.

Here's why someone with multiple ounces of gold might trade some gold for largents: as noted above, the trade in largents for other currencies and goods and services will naturally create opportunities to earn profits by taking advantage of premiums and discounts between the currency exchange rates and the price of goods and services.

To take but one example of many, suppose I own ten ounces of gold and decide to trade one or two for profit. Let's say gold fetches $1,200 per ounce priced in dollars and 1,500 when priced in largents—a 25% premium. If the currency exchange premium between dollars and largents is 15%, I can earn a quick 10% by selling an ounce of gold for largents and then converting the largents into dollars. If there is a 20% discount being offered on goods sold in largents, I can use the proceeds from selling the gold to buy goods in largents that I can then resell for dollars for as much as a 30% gain (10% from the sale of the gold after exchanging the proceeds into dollars, and the 20% gain from buying goods in largents and selling them in dollars).

In effect, by trading gold for largents I now have 20% of an ounce of gold as my profit.

In general, we can anticipate the discount offered for goods and services in largents will decline as the global marketplace expands. The hefty profit available to early adopters incentivizes the rapid adoption of the largent-priced marketplace.

The Airline Frequent-Flyer Mileage Model

Skeptics of the labor-backed largent model naturally alight on inflation/loss of purchasing power as the problem with digital currencies unbacked by gold or other commodities. These skeptics anticipate that the largents will be created far in excess of the demand for the currency, and the purchasing power of the largent will plummet to near-zero.

I have shown in the above examples that there are countless businesses with surplus goods and services they cannot sell for a profit in the current overcapacity-burdened global market. For example, a lumber yard with ten sheets of plywood damaged in delivery might be able to get full price if they sell those damaged but still useful sheets in the CLIME marketplace and accept largents. A private taxi or Uber driver sitting idly with no customers might productively add customers if he accepts largents. The list of enterprises with surplus goods and labor sitting unproductively idle is long indeed.

Customers with cash are scarce in the global economy. The CLIME system introduces a vast new customer base with cash to spend on goods and services that are scarce in their community.

But the market for largents is not the only tool available to the system to maintain purchasing power. As noted in Section 1, money has two functions: a store of value and a means of exchange. The largent is not intended to serve as a store of value; it is only intended to serve as a means of exchange that facilitates the production and trade of goods and services. Put another way, the largent is designed to encourage a high rate of *money velocity*, the rate at which money facilitates trade.

Money that gathers dust in a potentate's vault has zero velocity; it just sits there. Money created by the central bank that sits in private banks as reserves also has a velocity of zero; both are *dead money*.

The largent price monitoring function yields a weekly or monthly snapshot of inflation within the CLIME system. If the purchasing power of largents is declining (and that can only happen if the supply of largents outstrips the expansion of goods and services available for sale or trade in the CLIME marketplace), the managing board of the CLIME system can depreciate the existing supply of largents on the model of airline frequent-flyer miles, which expire a few years after being issued. In economics, this controlled reduction in the purchasing power of currency is called *demurrage*.

In this model, a pre-announced percentage of largents that have remained untouched in accounts for two years are deleted from the system. As a result, the global supply of uncirculated largents will decrease. The remaining balance of untouched largents are deleted at the end of the third year.

This model of demurrage is dynamic, meaning that the time spans and percentages are adjusted to maintain the purchasing power of largents. The model deletes *dead-money* largents and encourages a rapid turnover of largents into goods and services, which are constantly being created by the labor of those earning largents.

In the above example, sellers of surplus goods in the global marketplace have no interest in socking largents away for years; they are motivated to convert largents into goods and services or other currencies immediately.

The *use it or lose it* high velocity of largents generates demand for goods and services priced in largents, and this availability generates more demand for largents. This model is a self-reinforcing virtuous feedback of enlarging the market for goods and services in largents and expanding the demand for largents to be used for consumption and investment in productive assets.

Adopting the Largent as a National Currency

Though it may seem farfetched to those mired in conventional thinking, the benefits accruing to a national government that adopts the largent as its national currency are unmatchable.

As noted in Chapter Six (*The essential role of crisis in systemic change*), the most likely candidates for radical monetary experimentation are those nations that have been prostrated by the debauching of their home currencies by rampant central bank money-creation or Treasury money-printing.

An enlightened state would immediately gain irreplaceable advantages by adopting the largent as their national currency. Since the largent cannot be issued in excess by their central bank or Treasury, its value is stable globally. Since the largent is only issued in exchange for productive labor, the nation-in-crisis can start paying its employees and contractors with largents by simply joining the CLIME system *en masse*. And since there is already a global marketplace for goods and services priced in largents, and a stable exchange rate between largents and other currencies, the nation adopting the largent has immediate access to a global market for its own goods and services and access to essentials produced by others.

This adoption by a nation-state offers an advantage to the global CLIME system as well, in that it generates demand for largents to pay taxes to the state and for loans to rebuild a nation shattered by currency crises and financial mismanagement.

The adoption of the largent as the national currency by an enlightened national government is not that different from nations that have adopted the U.S. dollar as their national currency. The benefits of the largent far exceed those of the dollar, as largents are created in the local economy by the productive labor of its work force. There is no equivalent limit on the creation of money in any other currency.

Resistance from the Current World-System

Despite the many advantages the CLIME system offers to those who are already prospering in the current world-system, we can anticipate tremendous resistance to the adoption of the CLIME system from those who feel threatened by the adoption of a currency they do not control: private banks, central banks and central states. Nations with generous social welfare programs have no motivation to question centralized control of money and the economy. It is only when centralized control fails (or when they witness the success of CLIME in other nations) that people will be open to CLIME as an alternative.

Digital currencies such as bitcoin offer a template for how a new currency can take hold despite official resistance. Since the currency is distributed globally and accessed digitally, outright bans are difficult to enforce. In nations suffering a self-induced currency crisis, digital currencies such as bitcoin are adopted informally in day-to-day life as a means of conducting business.

Systemic crisis and breakdown opens doors to new solutions. CLIME does not require the dissolution of existing systems; as noted earlier, CLIME integrates well with central states and market economies, as it is ultimately a system that helps those who are not prospering in the current arrangement to secure a stable income and a means of building capital.

CLIME System Vulnerabilities

As a digital system, CLIME is vulnerable to hacking. Clearly, the system must spend considerable resources to protect its integrity, and maintain backup plans for decisive responses to successful hacks, such as complete re-sets of the largent system and reissuance of largents to accredited members and groups.

Criminal gangs, warlords and other exploitive groups can be expected to try to siphon off the income and wealth generated by CLIME groups. The first line of defense against predators and parasites is anonymous reporting by members to the system's global managerial bodies. The second line of defense is the automated fraud detection system that scans all transactions and freezes any beyond a limited size and number of transactions per account.

If every transaction above a modest amount is flagged and frozen for investigation, and every set of transactions that exceeds very low thresholds is flagged and frozen for investigation, it becomes very difficult to extract many largents from the system.

If a criminal gang demanded one largent from 1,000 members, for example, the large number of transactions in a short time span would trigger a freeze of the account collecting the money. If a thief managed to steal 10,000 largents from a group account, this large sum would immediately trigger a freeze.

The transaction reviewing software also performs basic forensic accounting. If a group account slowly accrues a balance of 10,000 largents, the multiple deposits over time are evidence the sum is legitimate. If a group account suddenly receives a single deposit of 10,000 largents, the lack of any history and the large sum trigger a freeze and investigation.

The third line of defense is the deletion of all largents held by unauthorized groups or suspicious accounts by nominally compliant groups. For example, any account that suddenly registers a balance of a million largents is instantly frozen. If investigation turns up fraud, theft, predation, etc., the money is deleted from the system: the ill-gotten money disappears forever.

Since this review of every transaction is automated, there is no way to spoof the system or bribe/threaten anyone into granting an privilege.

These lines of defense are not easily overcome, as they include both human reporting and automated software reviews. Once the news spreads that ill-gotten gains in largents can never be extracted or used, the attempts to plunder the system will likely diminish.

I claim no expertise in security, but very basic protections could be added to the system as needed. If encryption is not enough, a two-key system might be a solution, where a code unique to each member's device is required to approve a transaction from the member's account.

This approval process could even have a PIN code trip-line: one PIN code is used in normal transactions, and a second is used to flag a coerced transaction.

Since the system issues payments to those working to protect its integrity, very substantial resources can be assembled to protect the system from hackers and thieves. The power to erase illegitimate, counterfeit or stolen largents is a very powerful defense against fraud and theft that is unavailable to cash or precious-metals currencies.

The Limits and Promise of CLIME

The CLIME system has a number of limits that are self-evident. The CLIME system cannot restore order to a nation torn apart by warlords' military conflicts. It cannot reduce a totalitarian state that executes anyone who joins a CLIME group.

What CLIME can do is offer a model that enriches the lives and security of its members everywhere. The hope this model inspires may have political manifestations, as people shorn of hope within the current world system may demand the opportunity to launch CLIME groups in their communities.

Those in political power may realize that the risks of letting CLIME spread to their nation are far lower than the risks of social and political turmoil as poverty and rising inequality push the citizenry to dangerous extremes. As noted before, enlightened states—even if the enlightenment is driven by self-interest—would do well to actively promote the CLIME system as a means of alleviating the poverty of those who are not prospering in the current world system.

As previously marginalized people prosper, trade increases which eventually raises tax revenues. Rather than being a threat, the largent should be welcomed as a stable global currency that offers benefits to every nation that embraces the CLIME system.

CLIME: a New Narrative and a Radically Beneficial Way of Living

I have waited to the very end of this book to spring another philosophic word on you. *Ontology* is the study of the nature of being. *Ontological* refers to the core nature of a thing or concept; it is akin to *inherent,* but it carries the additional idea that the thing cannot be any different than it is.

I've discussed ontology in terms of systems: given the rules and inputs of the current world system, the only possible outputs are *concentrations of wealth, power and privilege*, the subversion of democracy, poverty and rising inequality. This is the ontology of the current system; *there are no other possible outputs* in a system of centralized money and hierarchies that protect privilege and incentivize maximizing private gain as the system's primary purpose.

Remember *teleology* from the Introduction? It's the end-point of a system, the destination defined by the rules and inputs. Given these rules and inputs, for the current world system there is *no other possible destination* other than *concentrations of wealth, power and privilege*, the subversion of democracy, fewer positive social roles, poverty and rising inequality.

No wonder the current narrative is incoherent. The system claims to value democracy and opportunity, but it undermines both by its very nature.

The CLIME system offers a new narrative, where work is no longer contingent on profit, privilege and centralized money borrowed into existence at the top of the wealth/power pyramid.

The CLIME system is based on *membership, not privilege*, for privilege is a form of systemic exploitation of the many to benefit the few.

The CLIME system is coherent: the incentives are aligned with its goals and rules.

In CLIME, democracy, freedom, security and opportunity are the system's machinery. It cannot function without them.

In CLIME, *paid work and the freedom to choose one's work are the only possible outputs of the system.* By using a labor-backed currency that isn't borrowed into existence, CLIME inverts the flow of wealth and power: instead of flowing to the top of the pyramid (as in the current world system), income and capital (the sources of wealth and power) flow to the bottom of the pyramid. CLIME benefits the many as the *only possible output of a system* that integrates money creation, labor and the community economy: the Community Labor Integrated Money Economy.

CLIME is a new form of symbolic capital that reorders the human experience into a *radically beneficial way of living*. CLIME is not merely a system for distributing work, money and resources; it is also a *moral universe* that reorders our management of work, capital, communities and the planet's resources.

Work is not just the earning of money. *Work is life.* The purpose and meaning of work is the purpose and meaning of life. In saying *the future belongs to work that's meaningful,* we're saying that work in the CLIME system is intrinsically meaningful because it is within the control of each individual, household and community.

In saying *the future belongs to work that's meaningful,* we're staking out a moral universe in which *work should be meaningful.* Whether it is profitable or maximizes private gain are secondary matters, not the only things that matter.

CLIME's *ontology of membership* returns humanity to its roots, to the social order we were designed to thrive in. CLIME boils down to this: if you don't like your choices of community and work, start your own community and choose a different range of work. No matter which group you choose, you'll be paid if you perform work that is meaningful to the community.

In CLIME, the individual and community always have a choice.

Collectively, we have a choice. We can cling to the current incoherent, self-destructive world system, or we can bring CLIME to life.

In a way, it really isn't a choice. Now that CLIME is available, *it is our moral obligation to bring it to life*.

Why is this so? It's very simple. Unlike the current system, *CLIME creates a radically beneficial world as its only possible output.*

Shall we self-destruct or create a radically beneficial world? The answer is self-evident: let's create a radically beneficial world, for it's now in our power to do so.

Charles Hugh Smith
Berkeley, California
October 2015

Made in the USA
Lexington, KY
18 November 2015